RAMBLES ROUND DONEGAL

RAMBLES ROUND DONEGAL

Patrick Campbell

MERCIER PRESS

MERCIER PRESS
PO Box 5, 5 French Church Street, Cork
16 Hume Street, Dublin 2

ISBN 1 85635 012 6

A CIP record is available for this book from the British Library.

10 9 8 7 6 5 4 3

Printed in Ireland by Colour Books Ltd.

CONTENTS

PREFACE

The chief purpose of this little guide from Lough Erne to Lough Swilly, is to help the traveller to 'read and relax'. When the limbs are stretched and resting, when the hunger and thirst are quenched, and while in the comfort of a pleasant lounge or by the fireside of a homely mountain cottage, our traveller can plan from its pages his tours for the following days.

As well as being a help and an interest to our welcome stranger, it is also set as a renewal of memories which time may have dimmed for our returned exiles, while once again in the silence of mountains, lakes, glens and rivers, they proudly tread that same ground where knights and nobles, chieftains and earls fought with heart and hand for faith and fatherland. In times gone by they carved for themselves a niche of fame in those dark days, and won for themselves praise by their deeds of valour.

So, in wandering down those lanes and boreens, we hope that this little guide may help and renew, as well as create many fond recollections in such places where memories fondly stray.

ACKNOWLEDGEMENTS

I am indebted to many friends who have given me much encouragement in the work of compiling "Rambles Round Donegal", to such trusted friends as Máiréad Reynolds, of the National Museum of Ireland, from whom I first got the encouragement to seek publication, to Dr. Kevin Danaher, Folklore Department, University College, Dublin, who encouraged me and my work to the publishers, to Miss Anne O'Dowd, Folk Life Division, National Museum of Ireland, for reading and revising this work, and to Pádraig Ó Snodaigh, Assistant Keeper of the Art and Industrial Division, National Museum.

I have in the persons of Breandán Mac Cnáimhsí and Seán Ó Lúing, Rannóg an Aistriúcháin, Leinster House, very dear friends who for many years, both of whom read this work and Breandán has given much help in translating Irish placenames.

I am most grateful to Mrs. Maureen Spain-Martin a very kind God-child who willingly undertook the drawing of the map and took much care in that task.

INTRODUCTION

Come with us along the highways and byways from the north-western shores of Lough Erne and coastward, between the heather and the sea around Donegal Bay and through the wildest corners of west Donegal, where you will always be among that same blue, brown, and purple of the mountains, and not far at any time from sleepy sounds, or the deafening roar of the breaking billows along that wild Atlantic coast. We shall cross mountain streams, the playground and haven of trout and salmon, and tramp those hills, and listen to the crow and call of snipe, grouse, and woodcock. The shrill call of the curlew harmonises with that lonely but restful peace. We will find ourselves among other charms that depend not on the mere beauty of glen, moor and mountain, or river, lake and sea, but among clinging memories and traditions.

Let us talk by the roadside or in the fields with men at work or meet fishermen as they come ashore; these will be some of one's best memories to look back on. Everywhere you will meet nothing but civility from a people who are friendly and willing to talk. Anyone who talks to the people on our way will find them for the most part cheerful company old and young. As yet the Ulster dialect will delight a student of speech and one will find many curious words and turns of phrase quite peculiar, which have perhaps filtered through the centuries since Elizabethan times.

For the ordinary holiday-maker with the ordinary amount of money to spend, and who seeks his pleasure in outdoor exertion, there is no better place in these islands or on the continent for that matter. Throughout the county Donegal the roads are good for the motorist and the cyclist; bus transport is always available, and there are good hotels in plenty. The north-west coastline of Tyrconnell is no longer a desolate place. Homes have been modernised and made comfortable and, though some parts may still seem stormbeaten and bleak to the stranger, those

9

winds have no cruel edge, but blow fresh and soft in from the Atlantic. This is a coastline and country much beloved, to which exiles gladly return with throbbing hearts from distant lands, and a haven where the emigrant's mind is in lifelong anchorage.

It will, I hope, make our coastal tour much more interesting if we have a glimpse here and there into the historical background of the places we may traverse through, and have a few words on the culture and industrial developments of those varied and different places. Like the colouring of the sea and sky over Tyrconnell, the ways, dialogue and customs of the folk of those districts are just as changeable. Their sayings, their ways of speech, and their different methods of work, which agree with the various types of land, give the visitor a variety seldom found in any other place in Europe. Such variety in dialogue, sayings and pattern of speech forever indicate to the 'local returned' or the 'exile come home' the district to which such sayings belong. It is sad to think that in the 1970's, with the closing of the small country and mountain schools and the introduction of the urban comprehensive schools, such a refreshing variety of identification has come to an end. Folk-life will be from now on so much the poorer.

LOUGH ERNE AND BALLYSHANNON

Towards the end of the last century a steamer was the mode of transport from Enniskillen to Castle Caldwell, for those visitors who wished to have a close up view of the twenty three miles of Lough Erne. This trip took two and a half hours, but I cannot think of two and a half hours of greater pleasure than sailing and treading your way along those clear waters, viewing the innumerable islets, and tasting the beauty of the surrounding country and hills. The Dublin bus route takes visitors along the south-western shores of the lake in recent years, where glimpses of those islands famous in song and story, in legend and history, are still unchanged. These are sites where holy men prayed and studied as seen by the monastic ruins and archaeological

10

finds, some of which are now in our national collection in the National Museum. Back in the great days of Tyrconnell, Lough Erne and most of its shores were under the O'Donnell's, while Enniskillen and the whole of Fermanagh were the Maguire country, and the Mac Clancy ruled from Lough Erne to Lough Melvin. To the north and north-east of Pettigo Sir Owen Gallagher was Lord, but subject to the O'Donnells. The river Erne was the O'Donnell's southern border, and across it ran the main thoroughfare from Connaught to Tyrconnell, passing through Bundoran and Ballyshannon. There was a time when every ford on the Erne river between Belleek and Asaroe had seen its battle, and old Ballyshannon on the river Erne was O'Donnell's frontier town and a place well marked in history. One of its most memorable events was the time of Red Hugh O'Donnell in July 1597, when Lord Burgh was making war upon Hugh O'Neill the great Earl of Tyrone. The Lord's marching orders were sent to Conyers Clifford who was then Governor of Connaught to attack Red Hugh, whereupon twenty two standards of foot and ten of cavalry marched through Sligo and northwards to the ford of Áth Cúl Uain half a mile below Belleek. Perhaps Lord Hugh Burgh thought that by crossing the O'Donnell country of Tyrconnell, O'Neill could be attacked from the north, or from the side where he had least prepared his defence. If such were the hopes of Burgh and Conyers Clifford, they had surprises coming to them.

In crossing the ford at Áth Cúl Uain, Murrough O'Brien ancestor to Lord Inchiquin was killed and the monks from the Abbey at Asaroe found his body. After they had interred it, the Franciscans in Donegal claimed that the O'Briens were all buried in their care and sought O'Brien's body. On Red Hugh's orders it was reinterred at the Abbey Donegal. The O'Donnells highly respected the bones of one descended from the lineage of Brian Boru. The troops of the Governor of Connaught had by now more in their noggin than they could sip. Even with fresh reinforcements from Galway sent by ship which had put into Inis Saimer, their big guns on Mullach na Sí were not having the desired effect on the

Castle of the O'Donnells. For three days heavy guns kept shooting at the Castle with heavy fiery balls of metal, and in thick and strong iron armour the choicest of Connaught's soldiers were sent to make resolute attacks on the fortress. All such attacks were of no avail; from the Castle were poured volleys of brilliant fire from well-planted straight-aimed guns which were at the ready within the fortress. Their covering guns provided little shelter or protection and great numbers of Clifford's troops were destroyed. Those who were wounded and exhausted were routed to the camp. Within three days the news of the battle had spread, and help was coming to Red Hugh's troops from Maguire of Fermanagh, O'Rourke of Breifne, and the Governor of Connaught's army was hard put to it between O'Donnell's sorties and the attacks from his helpers. Moreover all the fords were held from Lough Erne to the sea,

The Connaught troops were starving, and hungry men will risk anything. On the brink of the falls at Asaroe, a ford called Casán na gCuradh, (the Path of the Heroes) they crossed to the south side unperceived although many horses, women and wounded men, weakened by hunger, were swept over the falls and drowned. The stronger men got across. O'Donnell, very much annoyed that such a chance should have escaped his observation, followed the Connaught armies and running fights ensued from the Erne to Carbery. Little remains by the Erne to trace the castle, but as you cross over the bridge you can see the 'Path of the Heroes' just below you, and turning to the left you come to the side of Asaroe with its famous falls, and a dangerous ford, a spot one wouldn't like to face across. It is, however, a nice spot on a fine day when the river glitters and the sandhills cast their golden hue between you and the blue Atlantic. About other battles between Belleek and the sea, we will waste no more time except to mention that it is recorded that the Battle of Ballyshannon, as it was called, in which the Maguires of Fermanagh were involved with the forces of Her Majesty the Queen, took place on the 17th October, 1593 and here the early guns of the matchlock type were used; the man who made the

12

first one is unknown, and I feel he would indeed be happy to remain so, when one ponders over the blood spilt through such an invention. In this battle the English party was led by Captains Lee and Dowdall while the Maguires fought under their own chiefs.

BELLEEK POTTERY

Now to the visitors who are fortunate enough to have their own transport and can stop and start as they please, I would venture to suggest that a break at Belleek would be well worth while. Here you should pay a visit to the pottery where the well known Belleek ware is made. Just a brief history of the works may make such a visit that much more interesting. In 1857 this pottery was founded by David McBirney, a Dublin business man, and Robert Armstrong, architect of Royal Worcester works. Kaolin and feldspar had already been discovered on the river Erne, and inside three years the Belleek factory was making dinner, breakfast and toilet services in fine pottery bearing painted decoration. In 1863 William Bromley from Stoke-on-Trent turned out the first Parian china, and William Gallimore modelled figures, busts and statuettes which were shown from 1865 at exhibitions in Dublin. About the same time Henshall, also from Stoke, introduced porcelain basket making and flowering. Meanwhile, Mrs. William Armstrong — Anne Langley Nairn — designed and modelled the earliest and most beautiful ornamented porcelain. Her decorative subjects included those things which caught the eye in everyday life within the districts, such as seaweed, shells, rockwork, coral, sea urchins and so on. The material from Belleek became famous, because of its fineness, delicacy and its lustrous mother-of-pearl glaze. We should spend a little more time in Ballyshannon, (Béal Átha Seanaidh — The Ford-entrance of the Hill-slope). It is one of Ireland's most ancient towns, and a place where many notable literary families lived such as the O'Clerys, three brothers of whom became famous for their work in the *Annals of the Four Masters*. William Connolly, Speaker of the Irish Parliament was also born here. He built 'Ireland's most beautiful house' – Castletown, Co. Kildare. However, I think the person who creates the fondest memories was the poet William Allingham. Here on The Mall the house where he was born in 1824 is identified by a plaque, and his grave can be seen in St. Anne's, Mullach na Sí. The bridge across the Erne is now named Allingham's Bridge, and a memorial to the poet at the Allied Irish Bank, where he took up his first job, still keeps his memory fresh.

ALLINGHAM'S 'BALLYSHANNY'

William was the son of a bank manager, and at first took after his father's profession, but later he left that, for a job in the customs; here he found more time for the poetry on which his mind and heart was set. He got to know famous poets and writers, such as Hunt, Patmore and Rossetti, and corresponded with them. Allingham loved the simple ways of the people of the town, and it is said of him that while he was a clerk in the customs, when on his evening walks he would listen to colleens at their cottage doors singing old rhymes and ballads which he would learn. Those which were broken or incomplete he would add to and those which were improper he would refine. He printed them on long strips of blue paper like old songs, making the paper edges decorative, and he either gave them away to friends and neighbours, or sold them around. William Allingham died at the age of 65 years in the year 1889, but he will not be forgotten in his native town which he so affectionately loved. This is what he said of it:

"The little town where I was born has a voice of its own,
low, solemn and persistent, humming through the air,
night and day, summer and winter.
Whenever I think of that town I seem to hear the voice.
The river which makes it rolls over rocky ledges into the
    tide.
Before spreads a great ocean in sunshine or storm;
behind stretches a many islanded lake.

14

On the south runs a wavy line of blue mountains;
and on the north, over green, rocky hills, rise peaks of
a more distant range.
The trees hide in glens or cluster near the river;
grey rocks and boulders lie scattered about the windy
pastures.
The sky arches wide over all, giving room to multitudes of
stars by night, and long processions of clouds blown from
the sea,
but also, in the childish memory where these pictures
live, to deeps of celestial blue in the endless days of
summer.
An odd, out-of-the way little town ours, on the extreme
western verge of Europe.
Our next neighbours, sunset way, being citizens of the
great new republic, which indeed to our imagination
seemed little, if at all, further off than England in
the opposite direction."

Allingham gave to Ballyshannon the affection one would
associate with a good mother or father towards their young-
est child and in his verses, *The winding banks of Erne*, he
calls it by the pet name, 'Ballyshanny'. This poem has ten
verses, each one emotional and exciting, and so sentimental
as to bring a tear to the eye. I include the first verse as an
encouragement to those who love to find the heart and soul
of an author expressed in his words.

"Adieu to Ballyshanny! where I was bred and born;
Go where I may, I'll think of you, as sure as night and
    morn;
The kindly spot, the friendly town, where everyone is
    known,
And not a face in all the place but partly seems my own;
There's not a house or window, there's not a field or hill,
But East or West, in foreign lands, I'll recollect them still.
I leave my warm heart with you, tho' my back I'm forced
    to turn,
So adieu to Ballyshanny on the winding banks of Erne.

15

Those words must have been almost sacred to William Allingham, but there we will have to leave his beloved Ballyshanny and the winding banks of Erne, much as we would like to linger longer. However, for those who would like to do a more detailed survey of the old town and its surroundings, there is ample accommodation for the visitor or traveller.

THE ROAD TO ROSSNOWLAGH

It is between eleven and twelve miles to Donegal town as we take the road that leads past Asaroe and keep as near as we can to the coast, for once you have sighted the Atlantic you will hardly care to turn away from its view. For those who have time on hand once we have travelled about half a mile from the town on the way to Donegal we can see the ruins of the old abbey on the left about a quarter of a mile off the main road. About three miles further down the river lie the remains of Kilbarron Castle, the home of the O'Clerys, authors of the Four Masters. Of this old building little remains. Along the Coolmore road we have some beautiful views seaward. We can view the Sligo coast-line on one side and on another the northern coast of Donegal Bay, as its massive waves smash themselves to spray against the immovable cliffs of Slieve League. About four miles from Ballyshannon we come to the little village of Coolmore, and as we pass through the village a side-road to the left brings us down on to the beautiful holiday resort of Rossnowlagh, with its mile long strand which you can cycle or drive on. You should be watchful though about the time of the return of the tide as heavy waves rush in especially under the cliffs on the Coolmore side, and in those days of our youth we were told by older local people to be careful of every ninth wave as this one dashed in with greater force than all the others here on the Rossnowlagh strand. There are good hotels nearby on the top of the cliffs, and you can procure refreshments and a good meal at the Sand House. In my teenage years I was hired as a servant boy in the near-by townland of Durnesh with very nice kindly people named

Morrows. About the hiring system of those days we will say something more when we reach Donegal town where the 'hiring market' was held. About Rossnowlagh I speak from my experiences of fifty years ago when, with my old bicycle, no byway or highway was then unknown to me. For those who have their own car or bicycle there is no need to return the same way in order to reach the main road to Donegal. The new line, as it was called, from the strand will shortcut this journey, and bring you onto the Donegal road about two miles further on. This road is much more level and saves climbing back up from the strand onto the Coolmore-Ballintra road again. If you talk with local people or indeed to visitors who have been to Rossnowlagh before, they will tell you not to leave this beauty spot without paying a visit to the local Museum at the Franciscan monastery. Here you will be welcomed by the good friars, who returned to Donegal after four hundred years, and here at Rossnowlagh built a beautiful church, a monastery, and a museum.

THE CATHACH

Ballymagroarty is to the east of Ballintra which we are passing through on our way to Donegal town. Here lived the family by the name of Mac Robhartaigh — MacGroarty who were the official keepers of *The Cathach* that Irish Relic of St. Colmcille preserved by the O'Donnells who were the heads of *Cineal Conaill* or the people of Tyrconnell. It is said that the chiefs of Tyrconnell had great faith in this relic of St. Colmcille and claimed that numerous victories were achieved through its presence on battlefields. It was not lawful to open it, but it was carried on the breast of a coarb or cleric who, to the best of his knowledge, was free from mortal sin, and he was sent thrice rightwise round the armies of Tyrconnell. From this custom it took its name — *The Cathach* (The Battler). Its shrine can be seen in the National Museum, Dublin.

With the exception of the village of Ballintra, the surrounding districts are very sparsely populated. It is a district of noted families such as the Hamiltons and here Mrs. Hamilton had her cottage industries to help and teach those willing to help themselves. We will tell you more about this noted family as we leave Ballintra and Brownhall their family home.

There were strange marks and impressions left around Donegal Bay after the Ice Age, and we will have a closer look at them as we travel along the Drumhome road on our way to Donegal Town. Such marks are now known as the Green Islands and the most prominent of these is St. Ernan's island. It is believed that after the last Ice Age, and the subsequent great thaw, great lumps of clay floated down from the surrounding Cruacha Gorma (The Blue Stacks) — those mountains surrounding the town — and lodged on the solid bed of the bay, as also did those many hillocks which surround its shores. St. Ernan's is named in honour of a monk, a disciple of St. Colmcille who later became Abbot of the monastery of Drumhome (the lands within the parishes of Ballintra, Rossnowlagh, Laghy and Donegal).

THE GREEN ISLANDS

A well wooded road through rich grazing lands passes through the little village of Drumhome. When I was a boy I sat on top of a load of sacks of corn with my father who was leaving it at the mill to be ground for oatmeal. We had come all the way from the foot of the Eglish mountains — over twelve miles in distance. That was in 1922 when I was eleven years of age. It was my first time to get the taste of cheese as we ate it while going along with our load of corn. Later on in the 1920's this same highway was to me a path of joy as a cyclist. I was hired in Rossnowlagh and while cycling home or returning to the farm of my employment, the delicious scent of trees and hedges on a May morning along this Drumhome road created for me a life long memory.

St. Ernan's island is draped with a variety of distinctive trees and many flowering shrubs, but back in the early nineteenth century it had just two little shrubs or bushes, a holly and a hawthorn. It is surrounded by a high wall locally called the 'Famine Wall'. When the tide is out you can travel for miles on firm sand, and view its beauty from various aspects. To the north of St. Ernan's, is the island Ballyboyle, and more southward lies Rooney's Island. Bell's island is separated from her companions by a deep channel which stretches from above Murvagh, and here there is a golf course of natural links, which embraces the mountain, moorland, forest and ocean. The air at Murvagh is indeed a tonic and after a game of golf, one can relax in the clear blue waters which ripple in on its strand, or enjoy a refreshing drink in very up-to-date taverns in the nearby village of Laghy.

THE STORY OF JOHN HAMILTON AND HIS ISLAND

According to George Seaver it was by chance that a dwelling house came to be built on St. Ernan's, and it owes its existence to a young land owner John Hamilton, one of that Brownhall family we spoke about earlier. John was born in 1800, and his parents died when he was as yet a boy. (One of his uncles was the Duke of Wellington). He became of age, and assumed control of property of 20,000 acres including the family ancestral estate at Brownhall, Ballintra. The family also owned several small islands on the south shore of Donegal Bay. He rented some of those islands which could be reached by foot when the tide was out to local farmers for sheep grazing. From here on let George Seaver tell a very interesting story of what can be achieved through a united effort for a good cause, under a leader whose direction is respected and followed by men of different views in religion and politics. This very interesting article appeared in the *Church of Ireland Gazette*, February, 1975. I enjoyed reading it, and I hope George will forgive my reprinting it again. It is such a good story it could not be told too often.

'In 1824 there was a dispute over grazing rights between two of Mr. Hamilton's tenants who had sheep grazing on

19

St. Ernan's, and young John Hamilton rode on horseback over from Brownhall to settle the dispute. It was a beautiful harvest day in September, the tide was in, and the sun was shining, the view was delightful. John settled the dispute by compensating the tenants and taking over the island as a site for a summer residence. He there and then sent the boatman back for a spade and cord or line and marked out the foundations for a cottage. Two wee bushes grew there, a holly and a hawthorn; nothing else grew there that was higher than grass. He made a garden close and planted a few trees, but so exposed was the island in windy weather that he was obliged to tie his cabbage plants to the ground, 'each rigged like a mast', to prevent them from being blown out of the soil. But the trees flourished beyond expectation, so that in later years, it required more work thinning them out, than it took planting them in.'

In 1826 Mr. Hamilton brought his young wife, who had been afflicted with chronic lung trouble, to the island for her health. Soon after moving, when his wife showed signs of recovering, he left Brownhall, where he had lived, and its revenues to his brother, and began to enlarge the island cottage to a substantial mansion of hewn stone imported from the Mountcharles freestone quarries at Drumkeelan on the north west side of the bay, and about twelve miles by road. He built high garden walls and an archway on the island, as well as a large school-house across the causeway at the foot of Muckros, a gardener's cottage beyond it on the other side, and a corn-mill which, though now in ruins, still provides a fine example of structural skill. But all these buildings on the mainland required the prior construction of a causeway. This was necessary initially to block the channel and deflect its current. Subsequently, with the addition of a jetty half way across it was possible to transport immense quantities of freestone ferried from the Mountcharles quay. The making of the causeway against long odds and after repeated failures, provides source material for a minor epic. Not only was it achieved with the labour of unskilled men armed with nothing but picks,

20

spades and barrows, but also as the united effort of adherents of opposed factions, Catholic and Protestant, some of them even Ribbonmen and Orangemen working alongside one another in friendly competition, drawn together by the simple affection and gratitude towards their landlord.

A large tablet on the causeway wall, erected by John Hamilton's tenants after his death, bears witness to 'the great mutual love that existed' between him and them, forged through times of 'bitter famine and pestilence' when 'not for the first time or last time he stood between them and death'; and to the fact that 'people, Roman Catholic and Proestant came in their hundreds to build this causeway, refusing all recompense'.

Mr. John Hamilton died at a ripe age in 1884, and the St. Ernan's property passed to his son-in-law, A. H. Foster of Bell's Isle, brother of the Speaker in the Irish House of Commons. When A. H. Foster's wife Arabella died in 1905, the property was advertised for sale. Bought by Henry Danby of Ballyshannon, it was again sold by his executors to Mr. C. F. Dean-Morgan, who succeeded to the title of Lord Muskerry in 1950. It was fortunate both for him and his wife and for the future of the home that they had made a friend of Mrs. P. E. Smyth of Donegal town, who superintended Lord Muskerry's household affairs after his wife's death and attended him in his last illness. He died in May 1954, having bequeathed the St. Ernan's property to his cousin, Miss A. E. B. West of Workingham. But she, with a home of her own and a sufficiency of worldly goods, decided to offer it as a gift to the Church of Ireland as a home for the retirement of clergy, as a conference centre and also as a guest house for all and sundry. It is in the latter sense that the home has built up, through the years, a clientele of old friends who come and go for longer or shorter periods. They continue to grow and by far the majority having come once, come again.

I hope that the reprinting of George Seaver's article may attract new friends, and whether they be old or young, they will be sure of a hearty welcome at St. Ernan's.

My last association with St. Ernan's was back in 1928–29 when, with a very good friend, the late Edward Martin of Garvagh, Townawilly, we built loads of auction hay in those meadows and carted it to Townawilly, a distance of around nine miles. Those were the times when men stood back and admired a well built and shapely load of hay, as a 'work of art' and a 'thing of beauty'. A tasty[1] farmer was proud to be a master of such a craft. We have hardly finished talking of St. Ernan's and the Green Islands when the town of Donegal comes upon us with a surprise. As we round a bend in the road and travel over a slight hill we are in view of the old Quay. This hasn't changed much since the days when we watched the coal boats coming to anchor at the old Quay wall where the stone steps led down to the sea. A coal boat in the 1920's created a fuss, and everyone around the town and near to the town who had an able horse, got the few bob to earn drawing the coal from the boat to the merchants' yards. The old anchor which lay for centuries in the mud, has now been placed on a pedestal of honour. It is said to have been left there by a French vessel which called during the days of Humbert, but beat a speedy retreat, leaving its anchor as a mark of history.

THE FORT OF THE FOREIGNERS

A short distance below the present quay wall are the ruins of the famous Franciscan friary where the Four Masters completed their work on the great manuscript of that name. Little is left of the abbey which was founded by Nuala O'Donnell and finished by Hugh O'Donnell and his wife Fionnuala who was a lady of the O'Brien house of Thomond in 1474. Happily an amount of the castle, the seat of the O'Donnells, still remains and shows off some magnificent architecture of the Jacobean style. The mantle-piece of stone preserved in the great banqueting hall bears the arms of the Brookes, for in 1610 the castle was given to Sir Basil Brooke and is an example of one of the many fruits for those loyal to the crown, and a reminder of the confiscation times. In 1593 another Hugh O'Donnell was

1. A neat, tidy farmer.

22

coming near the end of his time when an English force seized an island in Donegal Bay, occupied the abbey and pillaged the country for miles around. Young Red Hugh at that time had made his escape from Dublin Castle where he had been imprisoned for four years. He reached Ballyshannon, tired and exhausted. Nevertheless on hearing of the occupation and insult to the abbey, he gathered all the forces at his command and marched on Donegal quickly driving out the invaders. Just after that his father resigned the O'Donnell leadership in favour of his son Red Hugh, who together with O'Neill of Tyrone, levied war on the English. Inside of five years the English forces suffered some of their heaviest losses on Irish soil. In 1593 after negotiations for peace had failed (for O'Neill was by no means so determined in his policy as Red Hugh O'Donnell), O'Neill seemingly got sufficient satisfaction through temporary victories, while O'Donnell had his mind made up to make a clean sweep, and rid for ever English influence from Irish soil. However, the O'Neill army laid siege to an English fort on the Blackwater near Armagh. A strong army of 4,000 foot and 6,000 horse under Sir Henry Bagenal was sent to relieve the fort. O'Neill called on O'Donnell, and the forces met at Béal an Átha Buí (The Yellow Ford) on the Blackwater, and the result of this battle was the greatest defeat inflicted upon the English at any time in Ireland. An English account said that they lost thirteen valiant captains, and 1,500 common soldiers – many of them veterans. Bagenal himself died and the fort on the Blackwater was surrendered.

Strange how we have moved so far from Donegal town, but the history of persons and places leads you unconsciously so far from the place in question that you almost forget what you were talking and writing about. Here around this triangular space in the centre of the town we have excellent and very modern hotels and guest houses, where nice meals are always ready and awaiting to be served and for those who would like to stop over for sightseeing around the county or neighbouring counties, there is no better spot. Indeed Donegal town is the hub for every part of the county where the main routes meet like the spokes of a wheel. For an exile returning after years, or oldtimers like myself who remember the Diamond in the 1920's and earlier years, a surprise awaits us. Gone are the horse and donkey carts, the side cars and traps, which we used to see tilted up on their end with an animal tied to the wheel and kept satisfied with an armful of hay or a bag of oats. Gone also are the old air-gun shooting galleries, controlled by that great character good old Alex Connolly whom we pray is in heaven. The rostrums of the 'Canters' have also disappeared as did their second hand clothes stalls, their china and delph, pots and pans, shoes, socks and stockings and the women dealers with the sweet-smelling *dilisc* or dulse, that edible seaweed which so many of us liked so well because of its salted taste and which spread all around that healthy whiff of the sea. The second Friday of each month was the Donegal fair-day before the marts came into being, and Saturday of each week was the market-day. Those were the evenings when the noise and din of Alex and his marksmen, mingled with the shouts and calls of the 'canter's markets', gave to the Diamond that air of commerce and enjoyment. Motor cars have now packed that space where in those carefree days we met the relations and friends, the neighbours and maybe the sweethearts at that well known meeting place – The Diamond. A twenty five foot memorial stands now on the Diamond built of Mountcharles stone to the memory of the Four Masters and bears the names of those authors Michael O'Clery, Peregrine O'Clery, Fearfasa O'Mulconry and Peregrine Duignan.

THE HIRING MARKET

There were times during my teenage years when I approached that same market-place with rather more caution, those occasions being the Hiring Fairs of the 1920's, when mountain lads like myself engaged ourselves to work and live on farms for six month terms. The Hiring Fairs of those years fell on the 20th and the 27th of May and again on the 20th and 27th of November for the winter term. I

24

first heard the farmers' husky salute in May 1926 — 'Are you for hiring, and how much do you want for the six months?' Well, I was for hiring and accepted after hard bargaining fourteen pounds for the six months to the 20th of November. For twelve further terms I accepted that same fare which those farmers had to offer, until 1932 when I left Donegal and the farmers' homes. I have never been sorry for that hard start to life in those 1920's, and indeed many setbacks and difficulties which have come my way since those days were made light, by early experiences of life as a hired servant boy with Donegal farmers. We are encouraged while in the town of Donegal to visit St. Patrick's memorial church of the Four Masters, just on a little rise, off the main street. It was built of Barnesmore red granite and opened in 1935. It is a very beautiful building with sloping buttress in Celtic design and exquisite masonry work which does great credit to native materials. On the hill just behind the church you have full view of the Blue Stack (na Cruacha Gorma) range in horseshoe formation from Barnesmore Gap towards the north-east around to Binbane in the west. This range of mountains is well worth a close-up view, and their beauty and scenery will be something for the visitor to remember. It was in a town-land by their sloping braes that I first got my name seventy years ago. I often traversed those hills in my bare feet as we minded our mountain sheep, which were then the main source of our income. I have known and loved the ways, customs, and traditions of those mountain folk and their concern for one another, inherited from times that were hard, when kindred ties and common needs gave them that sense of sharing.

A LOSS TO FOLK LIFE

It makes us sad when we reflect on the loss of the identity of those hills of beauty, when every glen, hill, hollow and brook was known by its beautiful Irish name. But, with a big change in mountain farming methods in recent years and new industries in towns, the motor car ever ready at the mountain homes to take the young people to work in towns and the closing of the small mountain schools, the identity of those hills is fast-a-fading. With the passing of the older mountain men goes this knowledge of those mountains and hills and it will never be replaced. However, as visitors we need not at this point of time reflect on the sad aspect of passing ways and customs. It is sufficient to bring to the notice of local organisations this loss, so as something may be undertaken in preservation and conservation before all those folk ways are beyond the efforts of record and research. For those who love a nice brisk walk or a good hike, the lake district of Lough Eske and Townawilly offers one of the finest to be found. This is a hike full of wonder and beauty, where the perfume of the fir forests meets the freshness of the mountains, to give the hiker the delight of youth and energy. But for those whose spirit is willing but whose limbs have become rather stiff or weak, a motor drive around this lake and its scenic districts will be most rewarding. We can stop and pull in at vantage points where a prominent view of the three and a half miles of placid and clear waters of the lake can be seen and Island O'Donnell, said to have been used by the O'Donnells as an internment camp for some of their prisoners, is draped as always in its mantle of evergreen trees and shrubs. Here one seems to feel, as we come closer to the Cruacha Gorma, that this horse shoe formation close to Lough Eske, seems to cloister us off from the worry, toil and hurly-burly of the outside world. The angler will have arrived at his haven, where ready advice and help can be got locally, and consent obtained to fish to his heart's content.

LOUGH ESKE, EDREGOLE AND TOWNAWILLY

Lough Eske can be approached from either the north or south sides, as this fifteen miles of ring road brings you right around the lake. About the half way mark we can view the beauty of that old Castle and grounds of Ardnamona (the height of the turf). Here advice can be had about fishing arrangements and boats can be procured at reasonable fees. Here also one can enjoy a hearty meal amid old time surroundings, where natural courtesy has never to be sought after. Indeed homely accommodation is always available for those who have enough of urban life. Lough Eske or Éisc (the fishy lake) is one of the finest fishing grounds for that rare and beautiful little fish *charr*, but anglers would have to wait until the last weeks of October for this sport, when these golden-coloured fish of the salmon species make their annual visit to the south shore of the lake, and then can be caught in plenty with ordinary worm or slug bait. Seldom have fishermen caught them during summer months, as they keep to the deep waters in the centre and feed on the bed of the lake. But, towards the end of the harvest month, they give rise to great sport and supply some fine bags. In recent years many visiting fishermen have made a point of returning again in the autumn to Lough Eske for the *charr* fishing.

To the north of the lake we find that wild, rugged and beautiful townland Edregole (Idir Gabhail — between the splashes or falls, or between the forked rivers.) Here we come to the end of a road and the Cruacha Gorma take over. The Corraber river flows along the townland's south boundary and drains the legendary mountain lake — Lough Bhéal Seód into Lough Eske. Lough Bhéal Seód (the mouth of the jewels) is amid the Cruacha Gorma about 2,235 ft. above sea level. It is well worth a visit for those who are youthful and active and fond of mountain climbing. From Edregole the mountain climb takes about two hours so you should be prepared and wear good strong boots. It is no harm to carry an extra pair of socks, as there are some soft marshes on the way, and nothing takes so much from the pleasure of mountain climbing as a pair of wet feet. Carry also some food or at least a pocket-piece lest fog may come, and you could have to wait for a clearance, as nothing can be so dangerous as to keep walking when one has no idea of direction. It is advisable though, to have someone with you who had done this mountain trip before, or a mountain man with the knowledge of the hills would make your day most enjoyable. He would keep to the dry ground along the foot of the cliffs and therefore avoid those marshy patches, which are so holding and tiring. You will travel over shoulder after shoulder of mountain heights which look identical, and on the crest of each one you will meet breathtaking scenery. Looking south and far beneath, Lough Eske looks like a mirror, inlaid by Ardnamona's forest on its north side shore, while it reflects its light and brightness towards the east, magnifying the beauty of that lovely district, Townawilly (Tamhnach an Mhullaigh — The arable place of the height). In the distance you will see a broad landscape reaching from Donegal town to the very western corner of that spectacular mountain, Ben Bulben in Co. Sligo, and also more southwards that long range of Fermanagh mountains south of Lough Erne. The wonder of all comes when you least expect it as you top the last shoulder of mountain, and suddenly come in view of that fairylike lake, with its charming little island, which at once gives you the wish to explore it. On my last visit I spotted on the island a beautiful kingfisher, embued with all its lovely colouring and looking very happy with many charming mountain wild-bird friends. To describe the lake and its surroundings one has to dispatch oneself completely from the busy world which we know today. Here along this sandy silvery shore enclosed by mighty cliffs to the north and west of the lake, one looks around apprehensively lest someone is walking behind, as the echo of one's own footsteps resound, while the call of the cur-lew or the bleat of a horned sheep from those lofty cliffs emphasise this peaceful silence. Would that the troubled world of our present times might have recourse to peace such as this, or the breakneck rush on roads, in towns and cities stop for a little and feel this God-given tranquillity, or people who have to live and work in polluted surround-ings breathe once more such freshness, and feel such quiet-ness as is free to all on our blue hills.

THE MOUTH OF THE JEWELS

No one who has ever visited Lough Bhéal Seód has ever been frightened by the black cat that is supposed to guard the treasures or jewels which are said to be hidden there, but I just can imagine how frightening the 'mew' of a cat would seem in the stillness and silence of those surroundings. Indeed there may well be some substance in such a tale as that of Lough Bhéal Seód (Lake of the Jewels). Close by we have the old way known as Casán na mBráthar (The Path of the Brothers) which, we are told, is the short-cut through the mountains made by the friars of the order of St. Francis to lead from their abbey in Donegal town or their friary on the shore of Lough Eske, to teach in wayside schools in the Glenfin district north of the Cruacha Gorma. The name Lough Bhéal Seód might possibly date from 1593 when English raiders took over the abbey, and pillaged the countryside around. At this time the friars may well have made their escape with their sacred vessels and selected the lake, with its prominent island markings, as a hiding place for their treasures and given it the name Bhéal Seód. Perhaps there is something in this name. Who knows? Anyhow to its dark waters, its silvery shores and its enchanted island we say adieu and make our way back again towards Edregole to meet once more the road which we parted from.

Many travellers, visitors and hikers down the years have passed along this way and were so taken by the gentle mountain folk and those beautiful hills, lakes and valleys, that they returned again with camp and caravan to spend longer periods in those glens. No one has any worries about sites for camping no matter where you pitch your tent. However, if you cared to be polite and to ask for permission, I can right away vouch that you will get ready approval. It is also so well known that no one ever leaves those mountains hungry, as refreshments are always offered to the stranger or the friend. Behind such kindness there is tradition and mountain custom as old as the hills we are rambling through, but in our modern trend, it can only be understood by those who have studied or have intimate knowledge of the ways of mountain people. Mountain sheep farmers who, down the years spent much of their time on those hills minding their flocks of sheep, will tell you of certain places where hunger strikes with such weakening effect, that were it not for the pocket-piece which they carried, they would have died of hunger. Such places were known as the 'hungry grass', or in Irish *féar gorta*. Seldom has the traveller parted from the door of a mountain home without first receiving the offer to partake of the food available. There, indeed, you have at least one reason why hospitality and kindly mountain customs have lived so long.

THE MASS ROCK

Let us not part from the districts around Lough Eske without paying a visit to at least one of the old 'mass rocks', which still bear the Irish name *carraig an aifrinn* and remain as proof of the faith of our fathers. The one which comes to mind and which is most convenient to visit is in the townland of Galladoo (Guala Dubh – The Black Shoulders), near to the crossroad leading to Cornaveigh (Corr na bhFiach – The Height of the Ravens). It is on the Townawilly side of the lake. This indeed is an extraordinary rock and surroundings, and much in keeping with descriptions and writings of those penal times. Here is a remarkable sheltered hollow where the rock is situated, with the ground rising in rapid contours and where you can picture the lines of people with each one having a perfect view of the Sacred Offering. The closeness of the apex of this gallery gave the guardsmen the advantage of being able to see all ways around and of being able to communicate instantly with the celebrant of the Mass. It is not only to refresh our knowledge of those times of history that we step aside to look on this spot; the beauty of the scenic height is in itself ample reward for lingering a while. I'm sure it was one of the spots in Mary Anne Martin's mind when she composed the lovely verses – *The Shores of Sweet Lough Eske*:

'I see old Ard na Móna, just as I saw it then,
A painter's brush could not describe nor yet a poet's pen,
It was there upon some well-known height,
For hours at length I'd bask;
To feast my eyes on its green woods.
Reflected in Lough Eske.'

A MORNING IN SPRING

True to the traditions of her ancestors Mary Anne
Martin has kept in focus the ways and spirit of the people
of this district in her songs and poems. Long may she keep
it alive. I hope that this following little composition of a
Sunday morning in Spring 1975 will bring the reader's
attention to the pleasantness of a dander along that Townawilly road.

That very fine year 1975 had already on the first Sunday
of April begun to show its brilliance. Kathleen, my wife,
and myself had made our way for the weekend from Dublin,
and we were now among the Cruacha Gorma hills. Since we
left those hills in 1931, we had not been there since in the
springtime. Oh, indeed, we had been there in summer and
autumn, and we had spent many holidays there, but there
is something about spring in that hill and lake district of
Eglish, Lough Eske, Edregole and Barnesmore which lifts
one's mind from the doldrums to the sublime. It was a
clear, dry morning with a slight touch of frost which gave
a crispness to the morning air. The sun had already cast its
first rays over the Barnesmore mountains, and a white cloud
which had been resting on the high peak of Croaghconnelagh
(Cruach Connallach — Connall's mountain) had quickly
evaporated and disappeared.

From Townawilly we made our way towards Edregole.
The journey was something over two miles. We had planned
to be in time to meet a good friend, John Slevin, with his
mini-bus bringing the mountain neighbours to eleven o'clock
mass in the parish church, St. Mary's, Killymard. Walking
briskly along that winding, undulating, but well surfaced

31

road, facing north, the air was so clear that the niches in the high cliffs of the Cruacha Gorma seemed but arm's reach away. Those mountains looked so near. The waters of the lake were so still that the houses, fields and forest had cast their reflection as if floating on the waters and Island O'Donnell was draped as ever with its trees so green. Over this natural beauty was a peace and silence beyond imagination. Looking westward against a clear blue sky we spotted about forty wild geese flying in V-shape formation. They were at a great height, and losing no time in flight. As they passed over us we could hear their lonesome dialogue. We watched them with much interest until they disappeared from our view behind the high peaks of Cnoc Néill Mhóir (Big Neil's mountain). We wondered where they had planned their destination, perhaps on the clear waters of lovely Lough Finn. Conscious that we had to be in time for John Slevin and his mini-bus to bring us to the church we kept moving along. Happily we had some time on hand for we were tempted to stop at Glas a' Charabhám bridge and look over the parapet wall at that clear mountain stream making its way with slumbering sounds in the stillness of the morning, to join the lake about a quarter of a mile through the fields.

By this time McGinley's dog had ceased his barking. We had passed down to the hollow out of sight of his viewpoint on the stone ditch opposite the kitchen window. It was unusual for him to see strangers like ourselves moving towards the mountains on a Sunday morning. Little notice would he have taken were we going southwards, as the mass-goers who would be making their way in that direction for eleven o'clock mass in St. Agatha's, Clar. But mountain dogs express their lack of reason very loudly when they see someone going or moving contrary to custom. Ascending the rise in the road from the hollow at the old stone bridge, our attention was immediately drawn to the field on the right hand side of the road where we were to witness one of the glories of spring – a peaceful pastoral scene. In the field by the river near to a clump of furze in a cosy corner, a mother ewe was much concerned about her new-born lamb, which at this time was but a few minutes old and already making feeble efforts to stand on his wobbling little legs. His mother was fondly licking his curly coat as he made a gallant effort to stand for the first time. It would have been nice to have had more time to enjoy this lovable springtime scene, but John could not be expected to leave other church-goers late in order that our curiosity might be satisfied. So, off we had to go at a brisker pace. This was, sure enough, springtime at its best, away from polluted streets and bus fumes, away from noisy roads and the hurry-burry of business places and factories. There, amid the silence and peace of mountain and lake with those first signs of spring, is where the majesty and power of our Maker is seen more vividly than anywhere else I can think of. This is a district whose beauty inspires one to delve deeper into its traditions, its history and its folklore. It is a place where all travellers get a hearty welcome, where Scottish folk in our young years came in great numbers, where such peace can fill a vacuum created in a world of strife and worry, and where, for a while at any rate, we may forget the uncertainty of days ahead.

THE GAP OF BARNESMORE

Before returning to Donegal town again, let us not fail to go and see Barnesmore Gap — the big opening between Croaghconnelagh (Cruach Connallach — Connall's mountain) and Croaghonagh (Cruach Eoghanach — Owen's mountain). Here in this very fine mountain pass the traveller is absolutely shut in between these two great hills as he wends his way along a really excellent road that traverses the gap. These are rugged and gaunt grey mountains which, from a distance, give off a hue of blue, and for three miles on either side the traveller is between massive cliffs and yawning rents cut by streams racing down the mountains and falling into the noisy Lowerymore river. This river keeps company with the main road as far as Lough Eske where it joins the river Eske. A visit to 'Biddie's of Barnes' is also a treat, where the 'pub' with a family tradition reaches back for generations. It was here that the late Rose Callaghan had a welcome for all. Here you can sit by the old-time fire while the kettle boils and from the scrubbed counter in that kitchen-bar order your choicest drinks. Those who like a cup of tea or coffee have but to chat until the kettle boils. By the time you say goodbye you will be glad you called, for you have made more friends with those who love to drop in to say 'hello' at 'Biddie's of Barnes' – the pub in the Gap.

The Gap of Barnes is associated with St. Patrick who rested there with his little sodality of friends while on his first missionary journey through Connaught and Ulster. Patrick had crossed the Erne at Carbery in Sligo where Cairbre hadn't received him kindly. He then called on Conall (i.e. Conall Gulban) whose family were converted and received the saint's blessing. Patrick laid his hands on the head of Fergus, one of Conall's family, and said that of his lineage a youth would be born, that is Colmcille. The saint then made his way through Barnesmore Gap and northwards to the top of Cark mountain overlooking the Swilly. At the ford of the river Deele, which runs through Convoy, the axle of his chariot broke, and when mended, broke again. Then Patrick knew the sign, and said to his friends not to go any further as the land north of the river had no need for him for a son would be born there who would be called Colmcille. Patrick turned towards the east and went to Grianán of Aileach overlooking the Foyle and Swilly rivers and there baptised Eoghan, the founder of the *Cineal Eoghain*, and first Lord of Tír Eoghain (Tyrone).

In later times the excitement of the first train through Barnesmore Gap brought crowds from the surrounding districts to the top of Cruach Connallach (Conall's mountain) to have a good view of the wonder as it was then thought to have been. This was on 25th of April, 1882. It is believed that many of the older people regarded the top of the mountain as near enough to it to feel safe. Some of them thought that it was the fulfilment of Colmcille's prophecy that before the end of the world, Barnes Gap would be part of the trail of the *Muc Dhubh* (The Black Pig) – that omen of disaster. So, to older folk who believed a lot in tradition

34

and superstition, the first train through Barnesmore was hailed as the 'black pig', and the end of the world was not too far off. However, the life of that friendly rail service was 77 years. It ended on the 16th September, 1959, and the sorrow which accompanied the last locomotive could only be compared with the excitement and wonder at the first steam engine train through the Gap. Before leaving the gable at 'Biddies of Barnes', let us look along those sloping braes facing east in the townlands of Ardnawark (Ard an Amhairc — The Look-out Height) and Friars Bush (Tom na mBráthar — The Bush of the Friars). At Ardnawark we can picture the highway men or the 'Molly Maguires' in their time having a splendid view of all approaches to the Gap. Indeed in the early 1920's, during the struggle for Irish Independence, many men who were on the run sheltered and watched along those same slopes, and listened in that mountain silence for the distant sounds of Crossley tenders carrying those British auxiliaries — The Black and Tans. There is a legend connected with Friars Bush which says that Cromwell hanged two monks there in the 1640's during his dreaded reign. Near to the road — just beyond the 'Barne's Inn' we may notice Cloch an Turais (The stone of the pilgrimage or visit) where, we have been told, childless couples made visits, and prayed for the blessing of off-spring. Those same townlands enjoy the first rays of the summer's sun as it peeps over the Barnes mountains. I have many pleasant memories dating back to my youthful years in the 1920's of very kind and gentle friends in those neat, thatched, snow white mountain homes, studded amidst their heathery background. A new pattern has now emerged, and modern bungalows have sprung up, which indeed look so nice, but gone are the cobble stoned streets leading to the red painted half doors, across which the stranger, as the friend, was greeted with hearty welcomes and kindly farewells. In such rapidly changing circumstances we may well have missed the picture, and we may have failed to record those kindly friendly ways of such mountain homes, which in times to come we might be glad to have preserved. And so, with edged appetites, sharpened by the fresh Barnesmore air, we return over the seven miles to Donegal town again where, for a change, we do some window shopping, after having tasted the hotel menus, and satisfied the 'inner man'.

We will notice Magee and Co., that very old firm which has kept pace with modern technique and development, but has maintained the link with the past in spirit and in practice. This firm has still kept confidence in the wool carder, the spinner, the knitter and the hand weaver, and they are turning out Donegal tweeds as in former days. From the sheep's back to the wearer, be he across the world or across the street, Donegal tweeds are always at hand, and their spinners, knitters and weavers are part and parcel of a traditional craft from mountain homes throughout the county from time immemorial. There are pleasant hours to be spent around the town where local knowledge is one's best guide. This can be had in the form of pleasant chats and talks with the folk we meet at hotels, restaurants, or at a musical session in a singing bar. All will be ready to guide and speak about places where there are keen prices, and pleasant shopping. Even the 'bingo' fans are very well catered for, and for knowledge of the many sessions both in Donegal town itself and neighbouring towns, that pleasure and knowledge will also be readily forthcoming from local gossip.

AROUND THE BANK

It is a pity to be hurried from the town of Donegal as there are many places where pleasant hours can be spent. The castle and the old abbey are places worth some study and the restfulness of a nice walk along the bank of the Eske on the north side of the river is in itself so soothing. Here you can recline on seats placed in the shade of high trees along the river bank and read your book or write your letter, or listen to the lullaby of the passing waters of the river Eske as they join mother ocean a short distance further on. The north side of the Eske river is in the parish of Killymard

(Cill Uí Bhaird — The Church of Uí Bhaird). Here on the town boundary we have an ancient spa which is also a holy well. It is locally called 'Father Mick's Well' after Father Michael Kelly of Killymard parish who blessed the well in the 1880s. Stations were made here up to the middle of the 1930s especially for the cure of toothache. Pilgrims claimed that by visiting, praying and drinking from this well they found great relief.

As 'old man time' keeps moving along we will have to hit the highway again along the coast 'between the heather and the sea' as we head for Mountcharles, a charming little town with a population of around 400 inhabitants. It is about four miles from the town of Donegal and people come and go frequently as neighbours between these two towns. Mountcharles is delightfully situated, built on the side of a steep hill from the top of which a very fine view of the bay can be obtained and looking towards the north and north-west the hills and mountains from Sruhill and Eglish around to Binbane form a background circle which would be hard to equal for beauty.

MOUNTCHARLES, MACMANUS AND ETHNA CARBERY

The land along this sheltered district is very good and always produced good and early crops. It is in complete contrast to the shallow stony soil and poor mountain land around Barnesmore. Along the four miles between Donegal and Mountcharles, the new modern homes mix quite pleasingly with handsome farm houses and larger homes such as those of the Marquis of Conyngham and that homestead so beautifully situated at Rossylangan which had been for long associated with the MacManus family. The MacManus's have been well-known for a long time in these two towns and the surrounding districts, and indeed further afield and beyond the Atlantic in the United States, where Séamus's stories of Donegal became best sellers.

Séamus MacManus was a school teacher until about 1898. He stopped teaching as he said he wasn't permitted to instill in his pupils a love for their native land under the educational system that existed at that time. 'I have always been kept as a third class teacher, and in schools where pupils could not reach third standard', he said. Séamus married the poetess Ethna Carbery, whose mother came from Donegal. Ethna was born in Belfast in the shadow of Cove Hill, but she loved Donegal and always claimed it as her home. Ethna has been described as an artist of great talent, a poet, a song-writer and a singer. A random quote from some of her verses shows much better the brightness in soul and mind of this lovable person:

'I know a purple moorland, where a blue loch lies,
Where a lonely plover circles and the peewit cries,
O, Do you yet remember that day in September,
The hills and shadowy waters beneath those tender skies.
Behind the scythes, swift lashing, a wealth of gold corn lay,
In every brake a singing voice had some sweet word to say,
When we took the track together across a world of heather,
With joy before us like a star to point the pleasant way.

In Kerry of the Kings you have the cuckoo call,
You watch the grouse grow withered, and its yellow glory fall,
Yet may some dream blow o'er you the welcome that's before you,
Among the wind swept heather, and grey glens of Donegal.'

For various reasons Séamus MacManus and Ethna Carbery have to be described together. Not only were they husband and wife but they both had a burning love for their native land. When Séamus left for America in the autumn of the year 1898, Ethna wrote the following as an expression of sorrow on the departure of her mountainy boy – the Páistín Fionn:

'O Pástín Fionn, but it vexed her sore,
The day you turned from your mother's door,
For the wide grey sea, and the strife and din,
that lie beyond, where the ships come in.'

38

However, no one was more overjoyed than Ethna was when, within eight months after his arrival in U.S.A., Séamus had got entrance to every leading magazine in America. He had successfully published his first American book, *A lad of the O'Friels*. That one and many others like *Knockagar* and *The Humours of Donegal*, enshrined in story forever tales like the 'Bonfire Night', 'The Pilgrimage to Lough Derg', and the 'American Wake'.

On the 2nd April, 1902, the voice of Ethna Carbery was silenced and her pen was stilled. She died at an early age, and in great sorrow Séamus MacManus, her husband wrote: 'The voice of the singer is silenced, the heart is stilled, the hand grown cold, and the lovable eyes closed forever. A light has been quenched in Éirinn, another hope has gone under the green sod. It was God's will. He knows best. Go ndéantar do thoil.' In the quiet village of Frosses, in the Catholic churchyard lies the remains of that well known and beloved Belfast poetess, writer and patriot, Ethna Carbery. Her husband, the Mountcharles born writer, is now interred in the same grave beneath the Celtic cross which he had erected to his wife's memory many years before. So ends our story of that lovable pair who were together in so many ways, and who were respected by all who knew them. Ethna's words of love can be found in her book of poems, *The Four Winds of Éireann*.

In the past, Donegal town, Mountcharles and the villages of Frosses and Inver were notable centres where Donegal hand embroidery work was distributed, and where mothers, wives and daughters collected it from agents and returned it at given times with the embroidery work finished and done. The returns for this fine, exacting needlework, in the early part of the present century averaged about one shilling and four pence a dozen for initialling or buttoning linen handkerchiefs. A miserable pittance, you may say, for such beautiful work. However, the 'spriggers', as they were called, were glad of those earnings, and in mountain homes where there were three or four daughters, it was a welcome income.

For members of An Óige who have come to Donegal and

who are anxious to stretch their limbs and rest, we should point out that Ball Hills, their camp, is but a short distance outside the town on the Mountcharles road and down by the sea. Here they can relax amid peaceful surroundings with good facilities for bathing, fishing, golfing and hiking. All along, this coastline offers good sea angling. For those who prefer fresh water fishing of brown trout, white trout or salmon, there are the Eske Fisheries, the Inver Fisheries, the St. Peter's and Golagh lakes and the rivers Eanymore and Bunlacky, to mention but a few. But, as I have mentioned before, you will be best advised through local roadside gossip, and meeting people at meals, or music sessions in pubs. It can be a major mistake for our visitors to keep strictly to the towns and main roads as much can be missed in sight-seeing of beauty spots which the general influx of visitors seldom experiences. I cannot think of a better place from which to explore the highways and byways than from any centre in or near to Mountcharles. To the north-west of the town we can branch off the Frosses road, and take the road to Letterbarrow which will eventually lead us right along the Eany valley to the Eglish and Sruhill Glens and to that spectacular mountain waterfall – the Grey Mare's Tail (Ruball na Lárach Báin). It is also known locally as the Scardán.

THE GREY MARE'S TAIL, ARDBAN SCHOOL AND SRUHILL

We can make side visits to places of interest either going to the mountains or on our return journey. Perhaps it would be more sensible to get to the mountains early in the day, and as twilight falls, we can make our acquaintances on the return journey with those places we noted on our way north-wards earlier. The road from Mountcharles to the Grey Mare's Tail is about nine miles. It passes by Letterbarrow post office where I collected my grandfather's old age pension, that large sum of five shillings a week. Later it was raised to seven and sixpence in the years after the 1914-1918 war. The wild woodbine cigarettes were then a penny halfpenny for a packet of five, but mountain lads going for the pension were not permitted to purchase cigarettes. In the summertime we wore no boots, which may be a reason why the old soles are still pliable.

In the townland of Ardban we can still see the little national school where I went to school. Its doors are closed, the sounds of those children's voices are no longer heard in the townland and I ask myself the many questions and seek in vain for the many answers which seem to call out loud for a reply:

'Where are all the scholars, those good friends, as well as those we fought with? Where are the little girls we passed the notes underneath the seats to? Where is that narrow gap which we wore out in the sod ditch, as we short-cutted our way to the school door each morning to make up those precious moments that saved our poor hands from the heavy black sally rod backed up by the power of a schoolmaster who was fierce and strong?' We had our political differences also. 'Where are the Sinn Feiners before that general election of 1918 who fought with those who wore that three leafed badge — that emblem of the Ancient Order of Hibernians — which displayed on each leaf the picture and names of those leaders — John Dillon, John Redmond and Joe Devlin?' I return my handkerchief to my coat pocket and close my jotter. The answers are not forthcoming.

From Ardban we turn right and cross the bridge over the Eany at Bun dá Abhann (The meeting of two rivers). We are now in the Parish of Killymard and here we enter the Eglish valley which is roughly three miles in length. This lovely hollow, where the tributaries from the Sruhill and Eglish mountains meet to form the Eanymore river, was a spot famous for its ghost stories. Such stories have lived with me, and even with a wisdom of seventy years, I can still experience those creepy feelings as darkness falls when near to Bun dá Abhann. How often when going to school we blessed the high floods in that river which had carried off the poles which were laid from bank to bank, and on which we crept across on going to school. This excuse was always accepted for school-missing, but about the mid

41

1920's a concrete bridge was built, and from that time on, other excuses had to be found.

MY OWN TOWNLAND

Now we pass through the townlands of Meenawilderg (Mín a' Bhaill Dheirg — Misk or field of the red spot), my native townland, and Meenatuggart (Mín a' tSagairt — Misk or field of the priest). When I was a boy there were ten neat three roomed, thatched, whitewashed homes by the side of the road. Large families were reared in each home, but as they grew up the hiring fairs and the emigrant ships beckoned to them, and they gradually left the glen. There are now only five of those side-of-the-road homes inhabited, while the ruins of the others point suspiciously to fifty five years of native government. A mile further ahead we enter the townland of Eglish (Eaglais — a church). Tradition has it that a wayside church beside a mountain stream passes under Eglish road. In this valley five families live and all have Ward or Mac a' Bháird for their surname. In years gone by there were eight families of the same name and the ruins of three homes are still to be seen. All the Wards were native Irish speakers and fear of any man never entered their minds. It was never possible that all of them could agree, until a time when any single one was attacked, and then all the Wards became united. It has been said that the Wards carried more marks after a harvest fair in Mountcharles long ago than the parish Christmas dues book had after their names. They believed that a man's best bodyguard was a blackthorn stick, a belief which has gone with the older Wards. I wouldn't dare to say so much about them if I hadn't been a half Ward myself, but apart from all that, they were the kindliest and friendliest of people, and no obligement to a neighbour was too great. With them a stranger was always welcomed. Seldom have I ever left the home or homes of the Wards without shedding a tear of gratitude for such gentle and good natured people as those in the townland of Eglish, that land of the Wards.

Here in Eglish we really have the tempting challenge for

the hiker, and the fisherman has but to step from the road as the river flows alongside it. The majestic cliffs and high spinks seem to come so near to meet and greet us and to invite us to their tops in order that we might see that amphitheatre of lakes dotted along like mystic mirrors with their streamlets racing over those cliffs, creating spectacular waterfalls on their way, and finally coming together in the valley far below to form the Eany river. The fascination of the pure and bracing breezes among those cliffs, and the heavenly peace of those Cruacha Gorma lend to that landscape charm and beauty which change at the will of cloud and sun, sending mighty shadows, and at times showers, along those emerald braes. It would be a great pity if such natural beauty and scenic wonder were despoiled by large plantations of fir trees. Forest planting can be overdone and large belts of trees will in years to come hide hills and houses along beauty spots like Eglish, Edregole and Banagher Hill, and transform their natural setting into an artificial environment. The line of the hills will be to a great extent spoiled by forest blotches and mountain homes will be deprived of a view which is at present enjoyed.

Quite apart from the landscape, Donegal mountain folk have customs which are surely all their own. In some ways they are rather shy and unassuming – traits which have, no doubt, been fostered down the centuries since Cromwellian days. They speak Irish and only rarely do they use the English language. In my own time I remember meeting people around the Cruacha Gorma who were so conscious of their poor English that they asked those who were more fluent in the language to do their private business for them, such as selling stock at markets and fairs. Such a feeling of inferiority was even noticeable in the parish church where the mountain people and the town people prayed at separate galleries. Seldom was a person from the town seen kneeling at the 'mountain gallery', as it was called, and never would a mountain person frequent the 'town gallery'. However, such a custom never created any real barrier to good friendship. It was something which the two communities accepted and perhaps never questioned.

But, times are changing and mountain folk are becoming less shy. They have always been generous and easy to make friends with, and one should never offer payment for what is freely given as such honesty might be taken by mountain people as an offence or an insult. Now that we have looked into the little 'fads' of nature in mountain folk we will retrace our steps for a few miles, and come on again to the road to Sruhill, that heart and soul of good natured mountain people. On our way we will pass by a famous turf bog in Clogher, which in my young years was used extensively by large farmers who came several miles to cut and save turf. Most of them employed mountain men to cut their turf, and paid them two shillings and sixpence per day. They claimed that a mountain man would cut more turf in one day than they themselves would cut in two days. They usually saved the turf themselves, and towards the harvest time it was not unusual to see up to ten horse loads of good black turf homeward bound, as the sun was sinking behind the hills. What a charming scene or picture this made, with fine well-groomed horses and bright red painted carts fitted with high turf creels, and well crivined[1] loads of good dry black turf. There was a contented look on each man's sun-tanned face, as he sat and smoked his pipe on a sack of hay on top of his load of turf, and listened to the hollow sound of cart-wheels as they rolled over the stone-surfaced road in the silence of an autumn evening.

After another two miles we come in view of the Grey Mare's Tail, that famous waterfall in the townland of Sruhill. Here also we have a gap or opening between two mountains — Bearna na Sruhaille.

A PENITENTIAL PILGRIMAGE

This opening resembles Barnesmore Gap, but without a road. Pilgrims travelled over the Sruhill mountains and through this mountain gap in their bare feet on penitential pilgrimage to a holy well, Doon Well, near Letterkenny. Fasting was part of the pilgrims' duties. They stopped in farmhouses for one night on the way to the well and returned

1. The crivin is the 'top' on a creel of turf.

44

on the third day, having covered up to ninety miles altogether. One of these bare-foot pilgrims was the late lamented James McGroary. The last time I talked to him, he described his *turas* to Doon Well in company with his uncle Nohor Kenny and a cousin. James told me the full story in Irish and English and I was so sorry that I hadn't a tape-recorder at hand. In those days such visits of penance were taken very seriously, and the warning was always in mind — 'it is only by prayer and penance we can hope to reach the Kingdom of Heaven'. James gave me the whole story of their journey over Sruhill in bare feet, and empty stomachs; their reception at a farmhouse on the other side of the Cruacha Gorma, and the joy of returning home after such a penitential pilgrimage. James was born and reared in the townland of Owenboy (Abhainn Bhuí — The Yellow River) a townland which kisses the mountain to our right as we go northwards along the Ardban-Clogher road.

Those visitors who have mechanically propelled machines — motor cars, buses, motor bikes or even bicycles are now no better off than the rest of us on 'shank's mare' as from here on a world of wonder opens up to the hiker and the mountaineer. Many young people I know will love to camp in this mountain townland, and why not? I can tell you, those who may be interested, your camp site will cost you nothing. You are now among the gentlest of mountain people — most sincere and friendly, though unfortunately, their numbers have decreased somewhat since I first followed the sheep around these hills.

THE MEN OF THE CRUACHA GORMA

The menfolk were experts in sheep stock, and famous for their knowledge of those mountains and hills. Their sheep dogs only understood commands given in the Irish language, and like many other mountain districts in Donegal, it has never been known of anyone to leave Sruhill without refreshments in plenty. In the summers of the 1920's on Sunday evenings, I often witnessed a house full of visitors and sheep farmers, all enjoying the big bowls of good strong

45

tea and beautiful pot-oven cake, capped with the finest home-made butter. The big decorative bowl was filled so generously, that if you were to slip your spoon into it, you would have to seek the assistance of your knife to fish it out. Those were the times we enjoyed such refreshments which were given by people whose hearts were as big as their hills, those great people the Kennedys and Kennys of Sruhill, the *Gasúir Mórs* (The big boys).

Sitting by the window in the Kennedy home attention is drawn to the Scardán, that big waterfall on the north mountain in the Sruhill townland. This part of the townland north of the river has been locally called 'Far Sruhill'. Ruball na Lárach Báine, (The Grey Mare's Tail) which this fall resembles so much, begins its long journey from a mountain lake named Lough Eascartha which is tucked in a valley behind one of the high cliffs on the north Sruhill side. This cliff or spink is called the Cock of Sruhill or *Coileach na Sruthaille*. The stream from this lough runs in an irregular direction and spills over the cliff from a height of about 1,800 feet, and falls into another stream which runs southwest from Sruhill Gap. This waterfall can be seen from a considerable distance and while in spate sends a foam all along its precipitous course.

The green braes to each side of it, which are continually watered from its spray, give a pleasant freshness to that mountainside, and a tasty run for mountain rabbits which were always plentiful there. This is the early source of the Eanymore river which ends in Inver Bay and provides the earnest fisherman with many pleasant hours. It also, no doubt, made an impression on many an emigrant who left its shores and the feelings of these people can be felt in the words of the songwriter, Patrick Ramsey, in his song *The Banks of the Sweet Eanymore*.

'How can I dream of that dear place, as if it were for me,
The purling rills of Sruhill Hills, perhaps no more to see,
Its far away I deemed to stray across the western tide,
To view those hills and other rills far away from Eanny's side.'

46

Now let us bid adieu to Sruhill and make our way to Dysert, (Díseart – a wilderness). It is far from being a wilderness, however, and such an impression will fade as quickly as the mountain mists.

On our way we pass through the townland of Meenaguse, (Mín na Giúise – A misk of small islands). This is a high mountainous townland which commands a beautiful view of Donegal Bay and its many islands.

CARNAWEEN

The western side of this hill gives us a delightful view of Carnaween (Carn na nÉan – The Height of the birds), a picturesque mountain. On its rugged heights is a cromlech, and the storms of centuries have engraved a sandy image on its south-eastern face which from a distance looks like the shape of a giant. This is locally named *Finn Mac Cool*. From the summit of Carnaween an extensive view of the country is enjoyed where the eye can behold the beauty of hill and dell, mountains and sea, as far away as Nephin in Co. Mayo and Benbulben in Sligo and that long range of the Fermanagh hills.

It was customary in our young days to gather to the top of Carnaween on the first Sunday of June each year for a festival of music, singing and dancing where the long Sunday evening passed in joy, and while on the way home the valleys rang to the sounds of our latest songs. But, such mountain customs do not now entertain our youth any more, as more fashionable fare lures them to towns and villages, to the singing pubs, and far away dance halls.

Below in the Dysert Dell we can visit the holy well of St. Colmcille, an altar-stone, and an ancient graveyard said to reach back to pagan times. All are said to have been blessed by the saint, and strange to relate rats do not live in Dysert clay. Indeed, it is well known that rats will not inhabit any place where the clay from Dysert is kept, and for that reason alone Dysert clay has been taken all over the world. Even the June day will be much too short for the youthful hiker or mountain climber once he reaches the top of Carnaween.

Much knowledge can be gathered by listening to local men whom we regularly meet on those mountain slopes. With their dogs and sticks we can rest with them on a sloping rock in the sunshine and listen to those unspoiled sounds and the names of the places in view. We will meet Burkes, Gallaghers, perhaps McHughs or Fureys who will tell you by Irish name every hill and hollow, every stream and valley.

Let us linger by Carn until the sun is sinking behind the hills at Binbane further to the west, where the Blue Stacks (Cruacha Gorma) give way to the road to the Glenties, the Rosses and Gweedore, and while the grouse and moorfowl call their young to safety we can gaze on those long fading rays of the setting sun saying adieu to those lovely sleepy valleys along the glens of the Eanybeg river. We will remember them with affection through such attractive and well adopted names – Seskinatany (Seascan an tSamhaigh – Quagmire of the Sorrel), Cronacarkfree (Cró na gCearc Fraoich – Valley of the grouse), and Meentacor (Mínte Corra – Smooth misks).

DRUMKEELAN QUARRY

The hiker, the angler, and the mountain climber will not want to be hurried from such pleasant mountain surroundings, and such placid fishing lakes and streams, but those returning to base may have time to call and see the freestone quarries at Drumkeelan. Here famous stone-cutters and great artisans in stone have left their mark in many a building all over Ireland and across the Irish sea. The names Monaghan, Ward, and McGroarty immediately come to my mind as such families have had long associations with Drumkeelan and Mountcharles stone quarries.

It may not be generally known that a major portion of the stone work, especially the round columns and decorative stone work, of the National Institutions of Science and Art Dublin, was done with Drumkeelan-Mountcharles freestone. In the 1870's this stone was transported by boat around the north-east coast from Mountcharles quay to the North Wall, Dublin. The Mountcharles stone has a fine grain and it is easy to dress. It has been a great success in decorative stone work especially for interior use.

A number of years ago an ancient house was found at a depth of 16 feet by turfcutters in a bog near to Drumkeelan. It was made of wood and it was twelve foot square and nine foot high, with a flat roof. The framework consisted of large trunks of trees, and the joints were cemented with composition resembling tar or grease. The house rested on thick layers of sand and gravel spread on the bog. Beneath its foundation there were traces of a paved road which rested on sleepers of timber and there were numerous vestiges of domestic utensils found in several places around the building.

Nearer to Mountcharles let us stop at the little side boreen to the right at the bend before we come to the town. I can recall the few stone steps or stile which we used to cross the ditch, and the path or casan which led to the lake and well. In the 1920's stations were made on the feast day of Ss. Peter and Paul, June 29th, to this well and people came in carts, traps, and side-cars from many parts. The evidence was there to be seen, in the form of votive offerings of a great variety, as well as sticks and crutches, that were left by the well. The name of the station was *Turas Pheadair* and it was famous for the many cures attributed to it.

In June 1919 at the age of eight years I recall going to the station with my mother and an aunt on a Sunday evening in June. The weather was beautiful and Connie McGroary who is still alive, thank God, gave us a very pleasant drive with his beautiful bay pony, and newly varnished pony trap.

PETER'S WELL

The journey from our home in Meenawilderg was about six and a half miles. My mother and aunt brought a baby of two years with them – a neighbour's child, whose limbs were slighty deformed. In company with Connie all three of them made the station and said the rosaries around the well, and around the mounds of stones, throwing another small stone from the lake shore on to the mounds as they finished each decade of the rosary. While the adults prayed at the holy well for that deformed child, I amused myself throwing stones into the lake, and watching the ripples on its placid surface.

I am sure that this was the first great thrill of my life, that lovely summer evening making our way home again to the mountains, listening to the rhythm of that beautiful pony's feet, the shining harness and the pleasant odour of that newly varnished and tastefully lined trap. But, to crown it all, that child that the station was made for, is still alive and going strong. He is now over sixty years and has walked many a mile since my mother and aunt Margaret carried him to St. Peter's well, and no one would ever think that his parents and his aunts were then so concerned about his deformed legs. Before leaving St. Peter's well the child's legs were immersed in the lake waters as part of the station. Stations are still performed at St. Peter's holy well, Mountcharles, mostly by the older folk, but not to the same extent as in those times of the 1920's.

KILLYBEGS

After a well earned rest at Mountcharles, our next stop should be Killybegs (Na Cealla Beaga — The Little Churches). It was up to the present century called by the Irish speaking folk Na Cealla. On our way we pass through the quiet villages of Frosses, Inver, Ardaghey and Dunkineely. The distance is about fourteen miles. The sea is on your left and not far at any time from the main road with some fine views across Donegal Bay. In passing through those villages thoughts of times long since, come to mind — some joyful, some otherwise. The sadness in Inver after the drownings of its fishermen in the early years of the present century. The joys in Ardaghey in the 1920's when its famous flute and drum band paraded, and the pride in seeing it take its place in band parades of the Ancient Order of Hibernians which were usually held in different towns throughout the country

50

each year on the 15th of August. It was heart-lifting to hear them play that old march *The Conquering Heroes*.

Killybegs is a peaceful town where fishermen come and go and where the dialogue and chorus of the seagull forms part of the familiar sounds of that town on the sea. It was always the great fishing harbour of south-west Donegal and one time it was thought that it could be made a port of call for American ocean-going steamers. But this never happened. Its harbour has always kept Killybegs in touch with the outside world, and strange vessels have frequently called there.

Three great ships of the Armada were driven on to Streedagh Strand between Sligo and Bundoran, and another the Rata, under Don Alonzo de Leyva, broke from anchor and ran ashore. Her crew later embarked on the San Martin which was holding out against the storm. They met the Girona and Duquesa Santa Anna, and made northwards, but the storm was still westerly and the three were obliged to put into Killybegs. The ships again foundered. The crews — 2000 in number — got ashore with their arms. Here they received a welcome from Mac Swiney of Bannagh, lord of this part, and obtained refreshments and stores. Two of their vessels were patched up again and put to sea, abandoning the San Martin.

There was no better fortune ahead, for the Duquesa Santa Anna ran upon rocks in Glenagivney Bay west of Inishowen Head. De Leyva made his way from her and joined the Girona which lay at anchor in Mulroy or Sheephaven. They worked on her for a week to make her seaworthy and set sail for Scotland. On rounding the Antrim coast near the Giant's Causeway she ran on a rock and perished. Five of her crew were recovered by Sorley Boy Mac Donnell, Lord of Dunluce, with some butts of wine, and a few pieces of cannon which Mac Donnell mounted on his castle and refused to part with.

Another one of the Spanish ships was wrecked at a neighbouring point and eleven of that crew called on Sorley Boy — Lord Mac Donnell — who eventually got them off to Scotland. The La Trinidad Valencera went ashore in

Inishowen — O'Doherty's country. Most of that crew succeeded in landing and were well treated by the natives.

But, from history back to reality, and our visitors will find Killybegs a very neat and interesting town where good and comfortable accommodation can be readily found.

There are splendid facilities for those who enjoy sailing and great sport is provided for sea-anglers. On the west side of the harbour are the remains of a Franciscan friary built by the Mac Swiney of Bannagh.

It is an important centre of the herring fishery industry and much in the news in our Irish efforts for a fifty mile limit, and the preservation of fish stocks in Irish sea fishing grounds. Donegal carpets, manufactured at Killybegs, are highly regarded the world over and can be seen in the making at the factory in Killybegs.

Along our journey from Mountcharles to Killybegs there are several holy wells. On the sloping seaside at Fanaghans near Inver is St. Naul's well. The saint is said to have drawn the water from a rock. This was once a centre of great devotion with an annual pilgrimage. Even up to the 1940's the presence of votive offerings and discarded crutches and sticks were to be found at the well. There is another holy well dedicated to the same saint near Ardaghy Hill, but its sacredness is almost forgotten. St. Conall Caol's holy well is at Bruckless and pilgrimages are made to it from May 22nd to June 30th. Also in Killybegs, there was once a famous pilgrimage to the holy well of St. Catherine. A few people still visit this well on November 25th each year.

Fifty yards from this well on higher ground are the ruins of Cat Castle. A story is told of a ship arriving at port from distant land after undergoing a terrible journey at sea. Among the passengers was a bishop who gave thanks to God for their safe landing at Killybegs. Near to the landing place, the bishop discovered a well which he blessed and dedicated to St. Catherine of Egypt, and placed the village and district under her care. The next story told about this holy well dates from about 1850 when a Protestant rector named Lodge had the well filled up with earth. The next day a spring burst forth in his drawing room and flooded

52

his home. His terrified wife prevailed on him to open the well again which he gladly did. The well is generally cleaned on the eve of the feast of St. Catherine and put in decent order for the pilgrimage on the following day.

The reader may notice that I do not describe in much detail the districts west of Mountcharles. The reason is not a lack of interest. But, when I was a boy our means of transport were limited. Everyone had to walk, and we mountainy people rarely moved outside the parish mearings. Indeed, means of communication were also restricted and we were lucky if a newspaper reached us on a market evening. So, not knowing west Donegal half as well as I would like to, leaves me incapable of describing the area from Killybegs to Lough Swilly in any great detail.

A short distance inland from Killybegs we reach Awark More (Amharc Mór – Great View). The like of this scene is beyond description, and there are few like it in these islands. It is the main look-out of the cliffs of Bunglass which drop rapidly to the water's edge. Scregeither rises directly from the ocean's edge and Bunglass Bay's blue waters open out all around. But the essential thing to do is to see Slieve League and Glencolumbkille, Malin Beg and the caves at Muckros, and I wish I could name those many other places of beauty, but what I've said before still stands. In west Donegal – 'you have but to ask to receive', and local people are the best directors.

It has been advised by those who really enjoy sightseeing and have experiences of the beauty of Donegal mountains that the best way of getting full focus of Slieve League is by boat – time and weather permitting.

This great cliff scenery has been enjoyed from many aspects. Along its tracks, asses and ponies carried ladies to the very top in years gone by. The richness in colour of this massive face of rock is truly wonderful. There are different hues in its rock formation, mingled with stains of various metallic ores, and accumulations of washed-down clays and soil, where mosses and the oddest things grow in the oddest places. Truly a life's study for the enthusiastic botanist.

This is a picture surely done in many colours by the unquestionable hand of nature, and once you see it you will never forget it.

On the other side of this mountain is a high cliff which ranges from 1,000 to 2,000 feet, and part of this chopped ridge is called the One Man's Pass. The sea stretches round to Teelin harbour, and outwards to Donegal Bay, across which the Sligo mountains stand out in their hue of blue.

The venturesome mountaineer can see more closely the One Man Pass while returning to Bunglass, and that spink of 1,812 feet which drops sheer down to the sea. The other side is nearly as high again and 1,000 feet below there is a lonely cave. Not far off there is yet another holy well — the holy well of Aodh Mac Bricne. It is near to the top of Slieve League. The 10th of November is the Saint's feast day, and weather at that time of the year would certainly increase the indulgence for those whose penitential inclinations gave them the courage to fulfil the duties attached to the making of the station. But the urge to gain indulgences by such penitential duties in wintery weather has decreased in recent times, and so the pilgrimage to the well of Aodh Mac Bricne has almost come to an end on Slieve League mountain.

ON THE ROAD TO KILCAR AND CARRICK

At Muckros bay we can view the caves and marine chambers and the grand cliff rising straight from the sea to a height of 916 feet. Nearby is the very fine strand of Tarloar, while on all sides there is charming coast and cliff scenery. There are many folk tales of haunted houses along this road by the sea, between Killybegs and Kilcar, and older folk in the districts claim that there is not a lie in any of those tales.

The White Hare

One of these houses is said to have a visitor in the form of a white hare which never can be caught or shot. Near Fintragh there is a very well-known house and the story goes of a family being evicted from it by the landlord many years ago. Despite representations being made on their behalf by the local parish priest the evictions were carried out. On the morning of the evictions the lady of the house spat on the doorsteps and said the place would never again flourish, and despite the fact that it is a stately and fine building and has been tried as an attraction for tourists, the spell remains and the only money ever made on the house was made on its sale.

The girl who eloped

This girl wished to marry a fellow of whom her parents did not approve and so she decided to elope. On the night or early morning that she took flight, dressed in her wedding garments her coach-driver lost control of the horses, and horses, carriage and occupants went into a swamp on the site of a quarry and were all drowned. Ever since that time the stone quarry is noted for the ghost or unseen spirit, such as a bride in her wedding dress.

More recently a house had been built there and seemingly the frequency of the unseen is noted throughout the night by the ringing of the doorbell at intervals. If it is not answered the first time, the toilet flushes, even though the family are in bed and the kettle boils in the kitchen even though the occupants are still in their bedrooms. There is another account related of a bread-van driver whose horse stopped near the same place, and wouldn't move. The horse actually stood on his hind legs, while the sweat poured from him. This went on for some minutes, and then as if whatever frightened the animal had gone or vanished, the horse moved on in his usual way. Needless to say its master suffered from fright as well as the horse.

The Lovely Ball

In a townland known as the Glen, outside Kilcar, on the Carrick road, a child went missing for some days, and frantic efforts by her parents and neighbours to find her failed.

After several days of unease and worry to her parents the child returned unharmed, and when asked by her father and mother where she had been, she told them that she had been playing with the children in the mountains. She said that these children had a lovely ball, the likes of which she had never seen before. Needless to say her father and mother did not believe her and passed the whole thing off as childish fantasy. Some time later, the little girl again strayed to the hills and returned home within a few hours, again telling her mother of the children with the beautiful ball. The child then said she would ask these children if she might bring the ball home to let her mother and father see it, and sure enough the ball was brought home the next day. All the family were called into the kitchen to see the ball, and when all had seen this beautiful coloured ball, in the clapping of hands it at once disappeared before their eyes. From that time onwards the child was forbidden to go into the mountain behind their home, and as well her parents brought their little girl to the local parish priest who was in the parish at that time. This strange affair would have happened about 45 or 50 years ago.

The Music and Dance of the 'Little People' of 1976

In 1976 a car load of teenagers was coming home from a dance in Glencolumbkille. All of them were from Kilcar. They were coming along the Meenaveen road, when they saw in the distance an unusual light, and little folk making merry. As they drew nearer to the sight they stopped their car and listened to the music which resembled the sounds of Irish music. Suddenly they became quite frightened, and were glad as their car sped away from this place, and its mysterious inhabitants. They told their story to their families but no one believed them. However, some months later a local man was in this same place cutting turf, and raising his head from the work he was doing he saw a little man coming along the *brú*[1] of the bank riding on what appeared to be a fox. This little man said to him to gather up his tools and go home as quickly as his legs
1. *brú*, bank.

56

would carry him. So he jumped on his bike and made off for Carrick, where he reported his experiences to the guards.

Kilcar and Carrick are neat little towns, well placed amid mountains and sea, and from these places trips and excursions can be made all over the county. They are also good stops for fishermen where apart from sea fishing there are very good rivers and lakes all within easy distance of these towns. The gunmen also have lots of space, and grouse, snipe and woodcock can readily be raised, and good bags realised.

Carrick and Kilcar are great centres for home-spuns and back over the years when we depended so much on home-markets, these centres of those cottage industries stood in good stead to the mountain peasants. Nowadays, Donegal home-spuns are purchased the world over. Visitors are welcome at any of the factories, which are now equipped with modern techniques and good machinery, and they will be able to see those up-to-date methods of production. An Óige members can again rest at their hostel – The Red House. Teelin village is but a short distance off, and this was one of the earliest centres of the Donegal fishing industries which was developed by the Congested District Board in the 1880s. At the harbour, the Glen river meets the sea, and the waters around Teelin bay are rich fishing grounds. In years past the fish hawkers and cadgers bought their loads of fish there, and hawked them throughout the country on their donkey and pony cars. The shouts of these fish hawkers could be heard in the harvest time for miles around and everyone made their way to the road to purchase their fresh and beautiful fish.

TEELIN'S HOLY WELL TRADITION

At Teelin there was a deep veneration for the 'Well of the Holy Women' (Tobar na mBan Naoimh), and a *turas* is still made to it on the 'Bonfire Night', the eve of the feast of St. John. It often happened that pilgrims sat up until daylight on the feast day, praying all night at the well, and keeping a bonfire alight. Stations were also made there on the feast of Ss. Peter and Paul, the 29th June, which in years past was a church holyday. These holy women to whom this well was dedicated were locally known as Ciall, Tuigse, and Náire (Sense, Understanding and Modesty). They were reared at Rann na Caille, beside where the well is, and they became three nuns, and blessed this well. Older people of the district say there was but one *turas*, and that pilgrims travelled long distances. The station on the Bonfire Night suggests that this was originally a pagan place of worship which was christianised by early missionaries. It is said that the fishing fleets sailing out from Teelin Bay to the open sea lowered their sails in salute on passing Tobar na mBan Naoimh. Tradition says that one of the sisters is buried in Cladach na gCaorach (the strand of the sheep), and that the other two are buried at Roilig na mBan (the graveyard of the women). The well of the 'Fair Winds' is also at Teelin, and during a storm at sea, it was traditionally believed, that if this well was cleaned, the fishing boats would return safely, and that by the cleaning and respect for this holy water, favourable winds would speed the fishing fleets home.

Before leaving Teelin we should follow the course of the river Owenwee (Abhainn Bhuí – The Yellow River) and for the benefit of our fresh water fishing enthusiasts this river rates among the best in Co. Donegal. The scenery throughout its complete course is very wild and at places it is magnificent and grand. It rises at Leahan Mountain in Lough Aura and half a mile further on receives a stream from Lough Divna and Lough Una, and there on passes the base of Slieve League and so on into Teelin Bay. Even for the hiker this course of the Owenwee river constitutes a memorable journey and a beautiful mountain walk, where the varied sounds of this lonely stream amid shrubbery, trees and heather, takes one's mind from the doldrums to the sublime. Having seen Slieve League, Kilcar, Teelin and Carrick, it is our next duty to call and see Glencolumbkille and Glen Head. We can make an excursion for a day to the Glen or we can go there and put up at a good hotel and perhaps spend a week. We could rent a thatched cottage, with every modern convenience at the Glencolumbkille Holiday Village. Here we can see the Folk Museum, the Folk Village or *clachan* which brings us back in time and which gives us an opportunity of seeing Donegal's cottage dwellings over a period of three centures. The *clachan*[1] is nestled close to a sheltering cliff as was customary in former times when such shelters broke the fury of the elements from both mountain and sea. Here we have the true cottage features, with domestic utensils and crafts- men's tools of the eras they represent. We can see the very poor home and living conditions of the cottier in 1720 with the limited space, the earthen floor, the settee and tester beds, the *cliabhán* or cradle, wooden vessels, spinning wheel and numerous other ways and features of those days and times.

The isolation of mountain and seacoast places such as Glencolumbkille in centuries past when there were few roads and little means of communciation, gave rise to the building of cottages in clusters, i.e. *clachan*, both for com- pany and protection in times of distress. We can see the marked improvement of the cottier's home in the 1820s, with its light by the single-wick paraffin lamp which took the place of the rush and tallow candles, and the chimney flue which gave a freshness to the living space which was hitherto polluted with turf-smoke from an open fire. There is an outshot built into the kitchen wall which gives addi- tional space and a much improved floor of stone flags replaces the earthen floor of earlier times. We can move on with time and see the very modern appearances of a cottage of the 1920s, with its good home-made table and chairs scrubbed clean, the shining bowls, plates and large dishes on the dresser and the churn and milk crocks by the side wall. At the end of the dresser hangs the *beetle* for making the potato *brúitín*, and bruising the potatoes in the big three-legged pot. Women folk will find much to attract them in knitwear and crochet, hand-knitting co-operatives, as well as hand embroidery. Basket making can also be seen, as well as brass and copper work, local marble, silver and goldsmith work and, by no means least, Donegal tweeds.

1. A cluster of houses.

59

This Glen of St. Colmcille is a wonderland all of its own. It has been made famous in recent years by the co-operation of its people with their dedicated and great pastor, Fr. James McDyer, a man who has studied every aspect of life on that wild and beautiful coast. Father McDyer will long be remembered for his whole-hearted and gallant work with his people, and the proof of their co-operation is there for all to see. This self-reliance, backed up by a communal effort in local enterprises, has created for them a love and a pride in their homeland, and in their own progress. It has to a great extent halted that trend to emigrate among those folk for whom, as Fr. McDyer himself says, 'emigration became a way of life'.

ARCHAEOLOGICAL RESEARCH

There is much evidence of the presence of man here in the Glen from very early times. There are many prehistoric monuments such as portal dolmens, souterrains, as well as cairns from the Bronze Age. There are twelve stone crosses all within a range of three miles in the Glen. Some of these have suffered from the weather of centuries and their designs are scarcely distinguishable, but all of them are venerated and respected. There are also the ruins of St. Colmcille's chapel on the hillside and an artificial underground passage which was discovered by men digging a grave in the cemetery of the Protestant church about eighty years ago. This passage or tunnel connected underground rooms, and its roof was made of large transverse stone flags. Such a passage gives an idea to the observer, that at one time or other people of the locality found it necessary to have recourse to such hiding places, most likely this would have been during the period of religious persecution, during the Penal Laws and when the right to practice their religion was denied to the Irish. There is much more to be said about Glencolumb-kille and its people, but I have not lived amongst them, so therefore I cannot write of them as I would of the folks I grew up with in the hills and glens around Eglish, Lough Eske and Barnesmore. I have met many from Glencolumbkille and I have found them the gentlest of people, amongst whom the stranger and visitor will feel at home, and be well briefed in all aspects of local recreation and history.

From the Glen we can go the short distance to Malin More and view Rathlin O'Byrne Island. The old coastguard station can also be seen there and near to the village are druidic remains at Cloghanmore. Here is a description of them from Mr. Cook's survey. 'Cloghanmore is an oval enclosure internally measuring forty-eight by thirty-six feet. At the west end are two double chambers roofed with enormous flags and traces of others adjoining. Two cells exist in the wall on opposite sides near the entrance. The enclosing wall is modern. On the opposite side of the road are two standing stones seven feet high and a fine cromlech'. Six more cromlechs (almost trop de luxe) 'are to be seen while through the village and another as we turn north towards the Glen'. Beyond the turn in the road, suddenly we see Glen Head, a mighty cliff with the wild sea breaking round its base, and sharp-edged rocks standing at an angle as if pieces were blown off them by some explosion. Wild indeed to the point of being startling, but wild and all as this Glen is it was the strange sanctuary of Ireland's greatest missionary St. Colmcille who founded so many monasteries in Ireland before exiling himself to work for God, and for further conversions on the lonely Island of Iona, amongst the Scottish and English. The mountains overlooking Glencolumbkille are plentifully populated in wild life, and birds of strange varieties can be seen everywhere between the mountains and the sea; one would have to be there in spring-time to fully enjoy the enchantment of their serenades, and birds' songs at eventide. It is indeed a haven of beauty and contentment to the enthusiastic naturalist.

TO THE GLENTIES AND ARDARA

From Carrick and Glencolumbkille our next stage should be Ardara and Glenties and for those who are fishing a good advice would be to make their stop at Ardara, which is six miles short of Glenties. Here they can enjoy fishing the

Owenea river which is very convenient, and one of the finest for good bags of fish and ranks high for salmon fishing. On the way to Ardara we meet Glengesh hill, probably the steepest piece of roadway in use in Ireland. Those on bicycles would do well to take warning to be careful at the top and the end of this twisted steep and dangerous mountain pass and anyhow you will want to dismount to enjoy this scenery. Ardara has always been a great centre of the hand-weaving industry. Along with other centres it received help from the Congested Districts Board and the Irish Industries Association, founded by Lady Aberdeen nearly one hundred years ago. These associations made many efforts to sell such materials in England, as well as hand-knitted garments, but their export efforts never gave great returns. They set up a great marketing centre in the town of Ardara and the Congested Districts Board, which took over from the Irish Industries Association, ensured through their expert examiners that each web and roll of home woven cloth was fully tested and tabbed. Such knitted garments and fine webs of home-woven material could be bought in shops all around the western towns of the county Donegal and even the hotels of those times also displayed such materials.

About 1879 Mrs. Ernest Hart started at Derrybeg, near Gweedore, classes for teaching the local people how to use native dyes which were at hand, such as lichen, heather, berries and peat-soot. Such colouring gave these garments a very acceptable appearance, and better looms raised the standard of the webs of materials. But, for those who would like to know more of the early days and of the spread of this great export trade which has developed so much in recent times, let us quote an account of the industry given by Mr. T.W. Rolleston who was secretary of the Irish Industries Association until the body ceased its years of volunteer work and left what it had begun to be carried further by the Congested Districts Board:

'If one could take a bird's eye view of this country, at an early hour in the morning, on the last day of any month, he could not fail to notice the number of persons, single or in groups, men and women, who are moving along these roads from every direction towards Ardara. Each wayfarer carries on his or her back a large and heavy bundle wrapped in a white cloth, and slung in a rope generally made of twisted rushes. Some of these travellers have risen in the middle of the night, and have perhaps walked these wild roads for hours under a storm of sleet or snow. When they arrive in Ardara the nature of their business is soon made clear. The white bundles contain each a big roll of homespun cloth, and they are bringing them to the Depot of the Congested Districts Board to be examined by the Inspector. Inside the Depot a scene of great activity is in progress. The tired peasant slings the big roll off his back, and straightens himself with relief as he gives his name and lays the cloth on the counter. Here two assistants take charge of it and begin rapidly to unroll it for examination. The man's name, the name of the townland where he lives, are entered on a label, which is attached to the piece of cloth. A duplicate label is handed to the owner, which he must produce when he comes to take his cloth away for sale in the Fair next morning. On the other side of the room there runs another long counter, before which the inspector stands, carefully scrutinizing the cloth which is pulled slowly along the counter before him. He is on the look out for faults, such as unevenness of width, or bars and streaks caused by irregularity in weaving. If the cloth is of good and uniform quality throughout, he places upon one corner of it a stamp composed of the letters C.D.B. (Congested Districts Board). The stamp carries with it a small award paid by the Board to the maker of the cloth.

The number of webs examined at each monthly inspection varies according to the season. When work is going on in the fields weaving is largely suspended. In the winter season the number sometimes exceeds one hundred — fifty, sixty, and seventy are usual returns. Each web will be worth, on an average, say £5 at first cost. It will be seen that the interest dealt with, although purely and solely a cottage industry carried on in the homes of the people, is one of considerable extent and it is one of vital importance to the inhabitants of this wild remote and barren region. The morning after the inspection, the first day of every month, the rolls of cloth are handed back to the owners, and if they have not been stamped, the nature of the faults and the proper remedy for them, which are recorded in the Inspection-book are pointed out. Patterns of new and saleable designs are also distributed to all who desire them. Then the Fair begins. The rolls of cloth are laid down on the footway, on both sides of the road; a great deal is brought in which was not finished in time for inspection; buyers are present from the neighbouring towns of Donegal, Killybegs and Glenties and there are several in Ardara itself. There is the usual bargaining and haggling; and Ardara, thronged with mountain folk, becomes for a time a Gaelic-speaking town. In two or three hours everything is disposed of and generally at good prices; for now that certain defects in workmanship have been overcome, this beautiful and unique fabric, stained with the soft, unfading colours produced by the people from common plants and mosses is in great demand.

Of the native dyes, those principally used are 'crotal' and heather. Crotal is the Irish name for the grey lichen that grows on granite and certain other rocks in boggy districts. Boiled down with the wool it yields a dye, varying according to the quantity used from a pale buff to a very dark red brown. Heather gives a bright yellow. Peat soot is used for a brownish yellow dye and the roots of the blackberry give a beautiful rich brown. Indigo and madder, which, of course, are bought in the shops are also much used. These colours are often combined to form other shades and a pretty varigated effect is obtained by a cunning admixture of little spots of pale-red or blue in the weft of a brown or fawn-coloured piece. A shade called 'silver grey' is produced by using a white warp with a weft of natural black wool. These webs are made from fine Shetland-like wool of a breed of sheep which are found towards the extremity of the penin-sula, about Malinmore. The other sheep of the district are mostly the black-faced Scotch sheep — hardy little animals with curly horns, which roam at will over the mountains and pick up a living like their owners, with much difficulty and hardship. As a rule, the owner of the raw material is not also the weaver. He clips his sheep; his wife and daughters card and spin the wool, and the yarn is then handed over to the weaver, who returns it in cloth and who is usually simply a peasant artizan, working for hire; though there are, of course, cases where the sheep owner is a weaver as well, or when a weaver will buy wool to make cloth for himself. The work of the Irish Industries Association in this region has been guided by Ruskins golden maxim: Ascertain what the people have been in the habit of doing, and encourage them to do that better: cherish above all things, local associations and hereditary skill.'

ON THE ROAD TO THE GLENTIES

It would be a great mistake to leave Ardara without travelling the six miles to that neat, clean and tidy town, Glenties, settled in the midst of the mountains with Cnoc an Airgid (Silver Hill) at its back; the town which four times captured the attention of Bord Fáilte's critics and won for itself and its residents that company's first prize for neatness and good taste. The town where Paddy Gallagher, better known as 'Paddy the Cope', set up one of his first 'co-ops' and had such faith in its people, as well as in his own town Dungloe. It is also the nearest town to the Glen of Glenties which gave birth to the man who said in his lines:

'Be merciful, kind,
And leave a name that will live behind,
At the certain end all men to bless
The man who is gone, for his righteousness,
And his seed will stand, sound to prevail,
And the name that he leaves will never fail.'

These words are from Patrick MacGill's poem 'The Rachary Wor'. Patrick MacGill — the socialist, the hired servant boy, the navvy, the librarian and the exile. Indeed he was a man who loved his mountain people and yearned to return, but it was not to be and Patrick died in a foreign land. Patrick MacGill the navvy poet, as he would like to be called, was born near to the town of Glenties in the year 1890. At twelve years of age he was hired with farmers along the Lagan for five pounds, ten shillings for six months of hard and slavish labour. Patrick was the eldest of eleven children to be reared on a small holding in that mountainous glen. Those were hard and scarce years for the mountain peasants and the mountain farmer would be well pleased were he able to have his debts all cleared by Christmas. After two years of hired service Patrick took the Derry boat, with others of his kinsfolk, to taste nothing sweeter than the 'tattee hocking' on Scottish farms. In telling of those experiences, Patrick said:

'They worked in gangs and lived under shameful conditions. We slept in barns and pig sties, often the cattle were turned out to make room for us . . . and we were paid 16 shillings a week, and our workday was no less than ten hours long.'

When this seasonal work came to an end MacGill took to the profession of the navvy, working at dam-building, tunnelling and experienced the lot of a builder's labourer. But be it with the dam-builders or plate-laying or while waiting to sleep in a barn or bothy, MacGill's pocket was never without a book and his mind was forever bent on the satisfaction of one day becoming educated and able to express himself through the written word. Each day as he finished his lunch-piece the book from his pocket came forth for the few minutes he had to spare. He studied foreign languages and joined circulating libraries in the districts of his work and made himself familiar with great writers.

Patrick MacGill's first effort at writing was the publication of his *Navvy's Scrapbook* and though it may have seemed childish it contained some poems which caught the notice of critics, here and in Britain. Literary mistakes didn't seem to curtain his genius and soon an invitation reached him from Mr. Pearson, editor of the *Daily Express*, asking him to join that paper's editorial staff. MacGill refused saying, 'although I may be a writer among navvies, I'm only

66

a navvy among writers'. However, Mr. Pearson kept insisting and finally MacGill accepted and left Glasgow for London to join the *Daily Express*. While working for the *Express*, he mixed with such men as G.K. Chesterton, Bernard Shaw, John Galsworthy and St. John Irvine. Patrick's work with the *Daily Express* did not always give him satisfaction, and general reporting routine, attending at shows and the like was far from the concern of MacGill, which was for the real needs of the time. The misery and want which he could see all around, made him come to dislike his work in Fleet Street – the headquarters of the *Daily Express*. MacGill's eagerness for learning had convinced many that lack of scholarship would never hinder his progress and his volumes of poetry, published by himself and printed by the *Derry Journal*, had made deep impressions on minds of literary people in high places. His verses, with boldness and fear associated with manual toil, were then very new and were a strong form of expression seldom heard before in English.

The publication of Patrick MacGill's first novel made his name renowned. He titled it *Children of the Dead End: The Autobiography of a Navvy*. Its success was tremendous, and it was described as the literary sensation of the year. After about a year came his book – *The Rat Pit*, which brought to light the terrible conditions of migratory workers on Scottish farms, but at the time little notice was taken and the government of the time paid little heed to the conditions which MacGill brought to light. The works of the navvy poet – the lad from Glenties Glen – had by this time taken their place on library shelves throughout Britain and the U.S.A. and the genius of the writer had created impressions which were significant among literary people in places as elevated as the Chapter Library at Windsor Castle, where Patrick MacGill was offered a post as an assistant to the learned Canon Dalton, ex-tutor of Princes Edward and George, domestic chaplain to Queen Victoria, Edward VII and George V. MacGill accepted the post. His appointment caused a sensation in the newspapers and headings and captions such as 'Romantic career of the navvy poet', 'The Donegal poet makes good', 'From the cow-byre to the

King's Castle', appeared. All this made his name better known, and his books became best sellers. Many publications from his pen followed the 1914-1918 war in which he took part with the London Irish. Amongst his works were *The Front* which dealt with the horrors of war as he himself experienced in the trenches, *The Great Push* which showed the London Irish and how they distinguished themselves in the battle of Loose, *The Amateur Soldier, Songs of Donegal* and his lovely little book *Glenmornan*. The last two gave much evidence of his great longings for a return to his native place but whatever other successes MacGill had, this was one which he did not achieve. He left England with his family in 1930 for the United States only intending to spend a short time there, but like many others from his native Donegal he never returned. An obituary notice in a local paper in the State of Massachusetts just told of his passing in the month of November, 1963.

> 'I'm going back to Glenties when the harvest fields are brown,
> And the Autumn sunset lingers on my little Irish town.
> When the grossamer is shining, where the moorland blossoms blow,
> I'll take the road across the hills I tramped so long ago —
> 'Tis far I am beyond the seas, but yearning voices call,
> Will you not come back to Glenties, and your wave-washed Donegal.'

One could talk and write for time on end about that gentle good-looking man, Patrick MacGill, but what makes one wonder is the fact that, in spite of the indifference with which his work was treated in Ireland, and indeed in his own county, he still loved the Irish and worshipped the people of his own Donegal always describing them as 'my own people'.

Just listen to the voices re-echoing in the mind of MacGill when he went about writing his novel, *The Rat Pit*.

'It's an hour before dawn — mid-winter — a cheerless morning, within the small hovel neither light nor warmth on the west coast of Donegal. The rushlight candle gone out, and the turf piled on the hearth refused to burn.

In the corner a woman coughed violently to the end of every breath in her body, then followed a struggle for renewed life. The battle against sickness went on in the darkness, and then two voices mingled with love and sadness.

The first voice —   'Have you your brogues, Nora?'
The second voice —   'They're tied around my shoulders with
                       a string, Mother.'
                      'And your brown penny for tea and
                       bread in the town, Nora.'
                      'It's in the corner of my weasel-skin
                       purse — mother'.
                      The tide is long on the turn, so you'd
                       better be off, Nora.'
                      'I'm off and away, mother.'

So, with those memories of Patrick MacGill, we move off from Glenties. It is now a more prosperous town than it was in MacGill's time. Indeed it is now a great centre of the hosiery industry and there are two factories working full time for export and the home market, making all that is best in Donegal knitwears. Just outside the town, about twenty five years ago, Bord na Móna opened up another thriving industry — the machine turf and peat production. From Glenties with the help of the most modern machines, the industrial and domestic needs of the northern counties can be supplied. The making of 'picture mouldings' are also a boom to Glenties and the well finished products in this industry have helped our export market.

ON OUR WAY TO DUNGLOE

On our way to Dungloe we will have to travel over a treeless mountain side, with a shifting panorama of brown crests and knolls with grey mists, and now and then a dim glimpse of the Atlantic. Coming near the end of this sixteen mile long journey and approaching the neighbourhood of

Dungloe, a cluster of little lakes comes in view, which gives good reason for the angler to feel satisfied, for these little lakes abound with brown and white trout. While in Dungloe the visitor can drive or cycle around the whole coast of the Rosses — which is a general name for the district north of Dungloe and on to Gweedore. Here the Atlantic breezes blow fresh, and with a wide variety of sport and amusements, and mixing with a homely people, the visitors' time will always be too short. Times have changed even in the Rosses since a traveller wrote this ditty.

'To reach it even a weary process
Toil awaits you 'ere you enter Rosses,
Between tides and strands and river fosses
Its ten to one if you land in Rosses.'

The roads today are very good and no one need have the fears of our eloquent friend of former times. The Rosses proper covers over sixty thousand acres including the whole parish of Templecrone. This whole district, from Inishfree Bay in the north, to the Gweebarra river in the south, and from Aran Island in the west to Loughanure and Slieve Sneachta mountain in the east, is a vast landscape of rock-strewn land which appeals to sportsmen and anglers. But even though this is chiefly a place of joy for the sportsman, it is by no means without interest to the non-sporting tourist.

That wonderously pretty Inishfree Bay is close by, as is the Spanish Rock on which there is good reason to believe one of the Armada ships was wrecked. In the early years of the present century a number of well-finished brass guns were recovered, but unfortunately they fell into wrong hands and were destroyed for scrap. We can drive around Cruit strand and see Cruit Island, and looking northward we can see The Stag Rocks, seven curious shaped pinnacles. Here indeed is much study for the keen geologist. According to legend these seven giants of rock at sea were supposed to have been seven ships which by enchantment, were changed into ocean rocks. In Termon peninsula we can look on the ruins of St. Crona's 7th century monastic foundation near which can be seen the Famine Wall and looking beyond the walls out to sea we can see the island where Napper Tandy landed in 1798. Having told you as much as I have learned myself of Dungloe and the Rosses, may I now bring you to the heart and soul of those good-natured people, through the first pages of Paddy Gallagher's (Paddy the Cope) book, *My Story*. This is a true life story set in the Rosses in the second half of the 19th century and well worth reading.

Paddy was born in the townland of Cleendra and says that he often heard that Neil Óg's house in the same townland was 'the highest house in Ireland'. 'Many a pleasant evening,' Paddy says, he spent in the same house, listening to Neil and his sister Máire telling stories.

'Hardly a day passes', Paddy tells, 'that there are not some of the Cleendra people standing or kneeling on the brae watching across the Atlantic. Some of the older people wondering why they cannot see their sons, daughters, brothers and sisters in that land across the ocean. There are no hills, mounts, forests or bushes between Cleendra and America.' 'Oh' sighs Paddy, 'if the naked eye could travel three hundred miles, wouldn't it be a grand sight.' Again Paddy tells us, if you are standing on Cleendra brae when there is a strong wind blowing from the west, the scenery is beautiful, the sea forming in rolls, about two hundred yards from the land, the rolls getting bigger, one after another; on and on they come, as if driven by some mechanical power; and as they come within twenty yards of the shore those big coils of blue water suddenly throw up a milky top and come dashing in against the rocks breaking into millions of little white bubbles. The cormorant and seagull rise happily on the waves, the sea pigeons fly out of the caves searching for a bit to eat, returning with a full belly. This was Paddy the Cope's description of his native townland in the Rosses, one of the one hundred and nine townlands which make up the Rosses district.

We are not far from the much spoken of Kerrytown where on January 11th, 1939, this district became famous as a result of a claim made by local people that the Blessed

71

Virgin was seen on several occasions. The apparitions of Our Lady, according to people who gave sworn evidence before a solicitor, occurred in the townland known as Meenbannad, and at set times in the years following 1939, pilgrims came from places as far away as Cork, Kerry, Belfast, Tipperary and England and Scotland. In one of the descriptions given after the first apparition an observer says:

"The Lady was very beautiful, and her face had a live complexion. She looked about 23 or 25 years of age. She wore a magnificent robe, and on her head, just over her brow she had a low wreath, such as a little girl wears on her First Communion Day. On her left arm, she held a lovely curly-haired baby. The figures were in an arch set into the Rock. This arch looked as if it were newly carved. The lady's feet were resting on a half circular block of what seemed to be lovely artificial material. This block had two carved mouldings, about three inches apart, running around it. I looked at the heavenly sight for some time and said to a companion, 'It is the Blessed Virgin'. My friend agreed, and said 'In God's Holy name, I'm going to speak to her', but in fright I said 'Leave well enough alone'."

A report was published in the *Irish Press* at that time and as a result of this report, people flocked to Kerrytown from all parts of Ireland. Further reports were published and then silence fell on Kerrytown. However, there is much evidence recorded that apparitions took place many times at this rock in the townland of Meenbannad and the parish priest of that time who at first did not believe in the apparitions later came to witness along with parishioners the vision on the rock; and again in 1942 as a Canon in the Catholic Church, he gave a further account of seeing an apparition in Kerrytown. In 1943 groups of people began to visit Kerrytown from Dublin and on the Feast of the Assumption in 1944 a statue of Our Lady of Lourdes, and an inscribed banner were carried in procession. The inscription which was embroidered across the top of the banner read — 'Dublin Honours Our Lady of the Stars at Kerrytown'. An image of Our Lady, surrounded by twelve stars was the centre piece, and beneath was the prayer, 'Mother of God, Queen of Ireland, Pray for us.' Pilgrimages continued throughout the 1950s and on August 15th, 1951, an unusual number of apparitions of Our Lady was reported.

A vision of a cross against a white background, and a golden monstrance containing a Host, was then claimed to have been seen by several people. A golden chalice, paten and Host were also seen ascending heavenwards on the right hand side of the 'Rock'. Some of the natives associated this phenomenon with the eviction and murdering of the monks from nearby Cruit island. It is claimed that the priest-hunters had driven them from their monastery, and having sheltered among the rocks of Kerrytown, they were finally hunted down and murdered at a place called Cill na Marbh, just at the rear of the house by the 'Rock'. That well known family that lived beside the 'Rock' had received many visitors since that night of January 11th, 1939, when members of the household were the first who claimed to have seen Our Lady. To accommodate the many pilgrims and invalids who came from far and near to pray here, the path from the main road to the 'Rock' was widened so that cars could convey the disabled to the place where the apparitions were seen. But, that home of the welcomes is now empty, the head of the house having died on the 23rd January 1952, and his wife six years later on 11th April, 1958. That friendly family are now sadly missed by those enquiring crowds that still come to pray at that 'Rock of the Visions', in the townland of Meenbannad, The Rosses, Co. Donegal.

Let us now call to that thriving seaside town of Burtonport which was always a great centre for the herring fishery and where coopering, net making and net mending gave welcome employment when times were hard. About one mile off the coast is Rutland Island, locally called Inis Mhic an Duirn. One time this was a place where improvements took place, with a custom-house, quays, stores, curing pans, a hotel, private houses and a military station. It was a centre of business life and activity, but its industry and commerce lasted but a short time and as the

73

sand storms buried Rosapenna on the shores of Sheephaven, so also did they blot out man's handiwork on Rutland Island. Talking of the islands, let us not leave these districts without crossing to Arranmore, where the fuschia blooms until well into September, and in most parts of the island the land is fertile and good for crops. In many corners of this, the largest of Donegal islands, there is an amount of timber, shrubbery and plants of many kinds which scent the salt-mixed air from off the Atlantic for the lifelong day. Anglers cannot go wrong and will be glad to know that rare rainbow trout can be caught here. But Arranmore, that isle of the tear and the smile, that joyous spot in the ocean, will long be remembered as the scene of one of our greatest Irish coastal disasters on November 9th, 1935. Many a boat had crossed those few miles of sea from Burtonport to Arranmore at every hour of the day and night, but on that fatal November night, a boat load of joyful harvesters returning from the potato picking on Scottish farms and carrying with them their small savings and joyfully looking forward to their homecoming welcome never returned. Nineteen of the Island's inhabitants were drowned within calling distance of their shore and only one survivor lived to tell that tragic story of joy turned to tragedy.

The young Gallagher boy of around thirty years survived that terrible night, and after care was able to remember how he grasped his father and a younger brother and held on to them. 'The others struggled in the waves and one by one disappeared in the darkness', he related. 'I kept hold of the keel of the upturned boat, still grasping my father and brother, but after about two hours or so my father was carried away by the terrible waves.' Gallagher still retained a grasp of his brother, and remained clutching the boat, until the awful tragedy was discovered at nine o'clock on Sunday morning. He had been sixteen hours struggling with those wild waves and his brother was then dead. He himself was taken from the sea in an exhausted condition by some of his neighbours and for over twenty

74

four hours he was unable to give an account of how the disaster occurred.

ARRANMORE IN SADNESS

"Lone, tearful Isle, you called your children home;
And none made answer from the morning sea,
Save one who tells such story of the night
As crushes his brave heart and crushes thee,
For those who sadly come with cold, dead face;
For those who come not yet nor hear thy voice.
Beneath those cruel waves that bore them full,
In youth's glad song, upon the piercing rock!
How sad to think thou coulds't have succoured them,
When death's dread vortex pulled thy dear one down.
But that you knew it not, nor heard their cry!
But that, unthinking, all your lights went out!

Dids't Thou not walk upon the waters, Lord,
When but a helm's half thrust had reached the shore?
Oh, foolish thought! Thy wondrous ways I see,
Take up the cross, I hear, and follow Me."

On several occasions since 1935 sea disasters around the Rosses coast have given cause for tears of grief. On May 10th, 1943, a mine floated into Ballymanus Bay where it exploded killing nineteen men and boys between the ages of fifteen and thirty-four years. Their names are inscribed on a memorial cross in Mullaghduff not far from the town of Dungloe. On 22 November, 1960, three of a crew of six were drowned when their boat struck a rock off Owey Island. On January 7th, 1975, the trawler *Evelyn Marie* sank off Rathlin O'Beirne Island and her crew of six perished. And on November 22nd, 1976, the *Carraig Úna* floundered off Rathlin O'Beirne Island and her crew of five was lost. While further back, on August 6th, 1914, just two days after the start of the 1914–1918 world war, the *H.M.S. Amphion* was sunk by the Germans off the Donegal coast. Lost off Tory Island on September 22nd, 1884, was the great gunship, *Wasp*, owned by the British Navy.

Now let us float on the waters and return again to Burtonport and back to Dungloe, where visitors would really be in luck to come at the time of the 'Mary of Dungloe', that international contest which is the highlight of a festival which is aimed to cater for everyone and timed usually to meet the peak holiday season. This is a well-organised and attractive programme of events and functions leading up to the selection of the queen for the honoured title — 'Mary from Dungloe'.

ON THE WAY TO GWEEDORE

The direct road from Dungloe to Gweedore (thirteen miles) crosses flat moor for the greater part, but the mountain ranges that are on your right, and the broken coast of many islets on the left, give an exciting view to every mile. We can pass the next little village of Annagry, where the thatched, neat, lime-washed cottage is still evident, but becoming out-numbered by more modern bungalows. We cross the Gweedore river at a spot where a combination of rock and waterfall make charming scenery. From Burtonport the road by Keadue strand could be followed and on to Kincasslagh and Mullaghderg where a good sized lake is separated only by a sand bank from the sea, and that giant Spanish Rock which keeps the memory of the wreck of a Spanish vessel which was thought to have been one of the Armada.

THE VALLEYS OF THE FINN, BARRA AND VEAGH

For the active visitors who are still around the Glenties and who wish to concentrate more on wild mountain scenery, there is no more exciting way than through the valleys of Lough Finn, Lough Barra, Lough Beag or Lough Veagh, all of which are off the beaten track. For highland scenery there is nothing in the county to surpass this course. Indeed excursions can be made from various centres on such mountain trips, and those taking part would be well advised to make an early start in the morning, as such places can crave you to linger, while those starting late may have to gallop all day, and feel sad by twilight in not having had more time to relax and enjoy such refreshing mountain peace.

"There is a beautiful lake in the Donegal Highlands
And long shall its memory remain in my mind,
Surpassing Lough Anna with holly crowned islands,
And borders of heath mids't beauty enshrined.
But its not for the beauty of lake stream or mountain
Which troubles my heart or the bosom within,
Its the parting of one, whom I loved with devotion
The bravest and best on the banks of Lough Finn."

Those taking off for the mountains from Glenties should keep to the Fintown road, and around the side of Knock-rawer, which can be seen from a distance. After five or six miles, a gentle incline, and then suddenly on to Lough Finn. This is a narrow stretch of water extending between three and four miles. On the south rises the high mountain of Aghla covered in dark heather and fast flowing streams; surely a grand place to sit and view even if one went there for that purpose alone.

THE FEAR GOWAN

There are stories told and songs sung about this legendary lake Lough Finn. One story goes that a youthful giant known by name as the Fear Gowan, lived some six miles north-west of the lake, and on a certain occasion while returning across the mountains to his home at Gleann Leithín from a visit to the south of Ireland, he was approached by a wild boar. The same wild beast had given fright to many along those lonely glens, and had overcome many a brave huntsman. The Fear Gowan was a young fearless huntsman, but on many occasions he was advised by his elder sister and Fenian friends to keep clear of those

77

runs which this fierce beast frequented. However, this young man was proud of his own ability as a huntsman, and he kept three great hunting dogs, in whom he placed great faith. He now, one day resolved to end this much feared-of beast, and took on himself to seek and find him and so ease for ever his neighbours' fears. So, over the mountains went the Fear Gowan, and his three dogs, and near the Head of Glenmore he made contact with the boar. A running encounter began, and continued through hills and glens on towards Lough Finn. The young Fenian believed that any one of his three dogs would make short work of the wild boar; so coming near to the lake he let go his first dog which attacked the boar fiercely and deliberately, but after a bloody struggle the boar got the better of the dog and left him dead on the mountain side. In like manner his second dog was killed, and then his last and most trustworthy dog was unleashed at the beast, who, by this time, was infuriated and blood-thirsty, and soon tore to pieces the last one of the Fear Gowan's trusted dogs.

The blood-thirsty boar now risen and mad turned on the young giant who bravely defended himself, retreating all the while down the steep slopes of Aghla, fighting with spear and stick until they reached the eastern bank of Lough Finn. By this time the boar was proving too able for the young giant, who now began to call for his loved sister, and his great voice seemed to shake the mountains and echoed across the hills. His sister heard him and came quickly towards the lake, filling her apron with large stones as she advanced along the lake shore. By the time she reached the lake her brother and the wild beast were both near their end. She could still hear her brother faintly calling, but owing to the echoes of the mountains she mistook the side of the lake from whence the shouts came. At a shallow end of the lake the sister waded across, but reaching the other side the calls seemed to come from the side she had left, so back again with her to find the same occurrences. Thus she kept crossing and recrossing the luckless lake, while all the time her brother's voice grew fainter, and gradually died out. After much crossing and searching in agonising anxiety the young giant's sister eventually came on her brother in a mass of torn flesh with the wild boar dead on the ground beside him. His dear sister, exhausted in her efforts to come to his relief, and anguished in mind at being too late to give her help, sank down and both died together about the same hour. Her name was Finna, hence the waters of that silent mountain lake bear a memorial to her faithfulness.

"Its not for the parting from lake, stream, or mountain
That troubles my heart or the bosom within,
Tis the parting of one whom I loved with devotion,
The bravest and best on the banks of Lough Finn."

Lough Finn is the source of the river Finn which flows eastward to Ballybofey and Stranorlar and from there on the same river meanders through the rich, flat and good arable lands of the Finn Valley where it joins up with the river Mourne at Lifford and both together form the Foyle and flow on to Derry. Near the Finn lake, is the neat little village called after it, and about four miles further on we come to Doochary. This is indeed a location of many attractions for the hiker, tourist or angler. 'It is only a step', as a mountain man would say, into the silent region of Lough Barra with its dark waters moving calmly under the Glendowan mountains and which on one side is surrounded with the shelving bank of white sand which frames those ink like waters into one of nature's extraordinary pictures. The mountaineer from this location can have some exciting climbing to reach the top of Slieve Sneachta, but Glendowan is an easier climb and both are rewarding with their magnificent views. Along the top of Slieve Sneachta the viewer can make his way until he can look down on the Poisoned Glen which is one of the finest scenic landscapes one would wish to gaze on. The great pass that crosses the Donegal Highlands from Gweebarra to Letterkenny can now be clearly seen, and almost parallel is the valley from Glenties to Fintown. Lough Gartan is also in view and hopefully we will see this again as it is such a nice centre for further excursions.

Behind the Derryveagh range the pass opens to Gweedore in line almost to Glenveagh, and as the visitor descends from those mountains his attention is drawn to that narrow still strip of water enclosed between the precipitous sides of Derryveagh and Glendowan mountains, the River Barra.

In 1857 a wealthy gentleman named John George Adair from Queen's County, which is now county Laois, became so enchanted and was so taken with the beauty of Glenveagh that he bought up the Gartan estates, an act which brought him into conflict with the mountain tenants. The sporting rights of those estates on which he claimed the right to hunt and shoot were disputed by Mr. James Johnston of Derryveagh, and a number of Mr. Johnston's tenants confronted Mr. Adair on the opening day of the shooting season in 1858 while with his dogs and gun he prepared to shoot over those estates. But Mr. Adair was determined at all costs to make himself master of all he possessed. For two years feelings and tempers ran high, and after many squabbles and allegations Mr. Adair served notice to quit on the Derryveagh tenants. In January 1860, Adair had written to both the parish priest and the Protestant rector of the locality, and claimed that he was attacked by a large armed party most of whom, he said, he knew as inhabitants. He was now telling in an aggravated manner of the demonstration made by a few tenants when he crossed the Derryveagh hills to assert his claim to shooting rights. He stocked the hills with sheep and claimed that many of them were killed by the tenants. Such accusations were freely made against the tenants and presentments were sent in by the grand jury, and a levy was issued on the district for compensation. The result was a great embittering of the relations between landlord and tenant. These poor mountain folk saw their goods distrained to pay for sheep which in all events could have died from other causes. This same gentleman who had stood for Parliament as a tenant-right candidate, and was said to be a kindly well-meaning man, was now determined under the guidance of a strong sense of duty to make an example of this community. Every effort was made to try to stop so dreadful a measure as to exile a community of several hundred. Even though may of the allegations made by Mr. Adair could not be fully substantiated, the sub-sheriff of the county nevertheless demanded an escort of 200 police and troops as well. On April 8th, 1861, the whole force moved on to work, and in a matter of three days had knocked down 28 houses, evicted 47 families, comprising 37 husbands, 35 wives, 159 children and 13 others making a total of 244 souls. As they hung around their levelled ruins, 50 were driven into the workhouse, one old man died from hardships he suffered, and two became insane.

Happily, however, the affair was so cruel as to excite notice both far and wide, and from far off Australia came the most sympathetic offer of relief. The Government of Victoria had offered free passages to all who cared to emigrate, and the greater part of those evicted accepted the offer.

Those are now far-off happenings, but before leaving the cliffs of Glenveagh it is our hope that an eagle, a hawk or a falcon might in their graceful movement float over those high mountains and come within eye's view of us. This part of the Donegal Highlands was forever noted for their presence, to the enchantment of many a visitor and the delight of numerous naturalists. It is a pity that preservation of those magnificent birds is not taken more seriously, for Glenveagh was one of their peaceful breeding places. I understand that occasionally the odd one can still be seen, but gamekeepers and large landowners of those mountain tracks had little time for such birds of prey no matter how graceful or beautiful they looked.

Indeed this wild mountain valley really gives nature a magnificent boost, where the slightest sounds resound, and in early summer the echo mocks the corncrake and the cuckoo, while the report from a gun, if fired near to the lake, is answered by a loud cracking noise, like as if the mountains were splitting to pieces. The Owencarrow river flows from Lough Veagh in the north-easterly direction on to Glen Lough, thence to the bright sandy shores of Rosguil. The Glenveagh bridge can be crossed and the road turns westward on by Kingarrow. On the north is Crocknalaragha and Muckish mountain while on the south is the great Dooish range which we have already seen from Glenveagh. Looking over all at the end of the valley is the unmistakable Errigal with its seams of white quartz glistening 'like the bright confines of another world'.

The tourist would be well advised to try to get to the top of Errigal mountain. Cars can drive to the foot of the mountain and those whose limbs are limber, will easily reach the peak in two hours. The loose shining shingle surface of white stones gives the top, from a distance, the appearance of a snow-capped Alp. 'Errigal the white Peak. Oh for a bright day!' Slieve Sneachta seems like an arm's length away, and the tops of the Derryveagh range can be seen. To the south clearly in view is Benbulben in Co. Sligo. Looking north-east one can feast one's eyes on the beauty of mountains in the counties of Tyrone and Derry, and as far away as Knocklayde in north-east Antrim, while if favoured with fine clear weather the Caledonian hills loom up in far away bonnie Scotland; with the aid of good glasses, this is a priceless view.

'Well so far so good' as the old saying goes, but before we are tried and tired of rugged mountainous sight-seeing we will call a halt at Gartan and there amid pleasant woodland, which follows the course of the Lannan river down to Ramelton, we will rest awhile. This is a good centre for the motorist, the cyclist, or indeed the hiker to do a survey of Gweedore, The Rock of Doon, Doon Well, Mulroy Bay, Kilmacrenan, and around the south end of the Swilly up to Letterkenny. Indeed, those with any kind of transport can easily spend a day on Tory Island and make it back again in time to sleep in Gartan. After a little relaxation around Gartan and its lovely lake, it would be well worth while to see Tory Island, though I never fancied the boat journey across and back. I seem always to be too cowardly of those stormy waters off our north-west coast. However, for those who like the challenge, the island is eight miles from the coast. It is almost three miles long and quite narrow with very little soil capable of producing crops of much purpose. Its population in times gone by was seventy to eighty families whose chief means of livelihood was fishing and kelp-making. On the island there was a neat chapel, a resident priest and a national school, as well as the lighthouse.

TORY AND 'BALOR OF THE MIGHTY BLOWS'

Tory is famed for its antiquities and traditions. Its people were very gentle and straight-forward, but lived much in ways which were handed down from times of the past. The rock scenery of the island coast is wild and lovely; the Fomorians lived there and erected a tower on the eastern side called Túr Conaing. Here the unwavering and mighty 'Balor of the mighty blows' had his headquarters. The legends of his exploits still live in the folklore of the island. He was its famous king who had one eye in the middle of his forehead and another directly opposite in the back of his head. The one at the back of his head had an overcoming power, and was kept closed, except when Balor wished to destroy an enemy or an adversary with it. A druid had foretold that Balor should be murdered by his own grandson, so for that reason he didn't intend to have a grandson, and locked up his only child, a daughter, in a tower built on the top of a cliff on the north-east side of the Island. Twelve matrons were left to care for her, with strict instruction to keep her from all intercourse with the outside world. Ethna, as she was named, grew to be a beautiful woman, and her father, feeling happily free in knowing that he had made her secure, as well as having overcome the predictions of the druid, took himself off at the head of a band of sea-rovers, pillaging the neighbouring coast, where a chief called MacKineely was the Lord of a large district. MacKineely, as well as being in love with Ethna, had much sympathy for her — locked up, as she was, in the lonely tower on Tory Island. He resolved to win her in marriage, and asked for the help of his friendly sprite, 'Biroge of the mountain'. Biroge dressed the chief in the robes of a young girl and sailed him across the sound to

83

the tower where Ethna was, and introduced her friend as a noble lady, just saved from a tyrant in an attempt to carry her off. Now she soon succeeded in introducing Ethna who accepted him as her husband.

In due course Ethna gave birth to three sons, whom Balor, her father, secured at once, and fastening them up in a sheet sent them out in a boat to be dropped to the deep. While crossing in the boat the pin which fastened the sheet gave way and one of the children fell into the water and disappeared; the other two were drowned at a spot known to this day as 'Port-a-delg'. The child who had fallen from the boat was carried off by Biroge and taken to his father, MacKineely, on the mainland. Balor, on hearing how the chief MacKineely deceived him, crossed from the island with a band of his fierce followers and succeeded in taking the chief a prisoner, and laying his head on a large white stone, he cut it off with one blow of his great sword. The stone with its red veins, tells of this bloody act, and gives its name to the neat little district of Cloghaneely (Cloch Cheann Fhaola).

The heir of MacKineely had in the meantime grown to be a powerful, able man, and having heard of the circumstances of his own birth and of his escape from drowning, as well as of his father's cruel death, he resolved to revenge. One day afterwards Balor called to a forge on the mainland where young MacKineely was also on business, and while in the course of conversation he remarked with pride of his victory over MacKineely, never thinking that he was now speaking to the son of his victim. The young chief filled with rage, watched for his chance, and reaching for a glowing red rod from the forge-furnace, thrust it through the basilisk eye of Balor, thus avenging his father's death, and fulfilling the prediction of the druid that Balor would be murdered by his own grandson.

A RETURN TO DONEGAL'S HOLY WELLS

The reader will see our subjects are as varied and as changeable as the picturesque highlands and sea-views which the traveller will enjoy in roaming the hills and glens of west and north-west Donegal. In such a journey between the heather and the sea, I would ask our friends to return with me briefly again to the ways of those prayerful folk of times gone by and visit some holy wells. A revival of such a grand old custom might again be within our reach, and when modern customs have not produced that much peace or happiness, a return to some old traditions could do no wrong. It would be a pity to pass by many more of Donegal's holy wells without at least recording them in such a traveller's hand-book. We have told you of holy wells from Donegal town to Slieve League, so now let us remember others along the west coast as far as we have travelled.

On Rathlin O'Beirne Island there is known to be a holy well and graveyard. The well is to the memory of St. Ciarán, St. Naul and St. Asieus of Elphin. A ruined chapel of St. Ciarán is at Malinbeg. Some called this holy well Tobar Rachlan, and devotion to this well was practiced up to ninety years ago. At Glencolumbkille there is a holy well and the saint's bed, the *turas*, is almost three miles long. This journey includes a climb up Cnoc a' Chuilinn and finishes at Glen Head. The well is near the winding pathway or *casán* and is sacred to the memory of the great saint as is the stone-bed which he is said to have used. There are two holy wells between Cashel and Meenacross very near to each other in the townland of Kilgoley. The wells are now without names, but cures are believed to have taken place at them. Still near to Glencolumbkille in the townland of Killaned and not far from Cashel national school, O'Donovan's letters say there was another chapel dedicated to the memory of St. Athnaid in the same Killaned townland. St. Athnaid's cell and roilig are near the well. In Dooey townland, not so far from the one mentioned, is Conall's Well (Tobar Chonaill) and beside it lies a flagstone which is believed to have cured many ailments. This flagstone was at one time taken to America because of its healing powers and was again returned. It is also recorded that there is a holy well on the north side of the Glen in the townland of Clochán.

West of Ardara on Loughros peninsula is Tobar Chonaill or St. Conall's Well. The *turas* went from the well around by Cloch Bhuidh, Drum Mortan, and Cill Chaisil. There is a holy well at Kiltoorish and the name seems to mean Church of the Pilgrimage. In Ardara parish, near the site of St. Shanaghan's Church, a very nice well can be found. It was venerated as St. Shanaghan's Well and up to recent years it was very well cared for. On Iniskeel Island can be found The Blessed Virgin's Well, and the well of St. Conall. Pilgrims went to St. Conall's well from May 22nd until September 12th. The Bell of St. Conall was brought to the island for veneration, and kissing the bell was part of the pilgrims' station duties. The bell was handed on from a family named Gearan who were thought to be caretakers of the monastery, and so it passed on until it came into the care of people who didn't fully attach so much importance to the relic, and it was sold about one hundred and twelve years ago. The Bell of St. Conall now rests in the British Museum. It is said that cattle and sheep bought by money received for the bell all died. St. Conall's holy well in Doochary is still remembered by the older folk in that district and there are some who still do the station there.

Dr. Maguire's History of the Diocese of Raphoe (p. 241) tells of a remarkable well in Dooey (near Lettermacaward) connected by tradition with St. Conall's first visit to those parts. The same history also tells of the holy well at Tarmon in Maghery south of Dungloe where *turas* was made up to recent years. In Dr. Maguire's history of the Diocese he also gives the method of making the turas. According to tradition there was once a monastery at Maghery and eleven bishops are buried there. Oileán Cróine has a Holy Well. This little island is off the coast of Templecrone in the parish of Cróine Beg. On Cruit Island there are three wells; Tobar Bhrighde (St. Brigid's Well), Tobar Mhuire (the Blessed Virgin's Well), and also a nameless well. Also on

Cruit can be found Leac Phroinsiais (St. Francis' flag-stone) which signifies that Cruit once contained a Franciscan foundation. Sick people, it is said, were brought to sleep on St. Francis's Leac, and those who slept were said to get better. Stations were made there on August 15th. At Calhame there is a holy well, a short distance from Mullaghduff national school. Stations were made there up to recent years, and at Cruck, south of the school, another well can be found. We find at Annagry, Tobar Naoimh Dubhthaigh, a holy well in honour of St. Dubhthach. There is a holy well at Bloody Foreland named Tobar Faoi Chnoc (Well under the hill). It is under Cnoc Fola. Some name it Tobar Ailt na Péiste. People passing by often say a prayer there. The tide comes over the well twice a day, but the water still remains fresh. Its earlier name is lost with the past generations.

On the shores of Ranafast can be found a holy well, Tobar na Spáinneach, and on the uninhabited island of Inishdooey between Inishbofin and Tory Island there is a holy well. The name of the island and well keeps alive the memory of St. Dubhthach whose feast is the 5th of February. Near Gortahork is found St. Colmcille's Well at a place called Arda Begga. Stations were made there on the saint's feast day, June 9th. There is a crude stone hammer among the stones at the well, which is regarded with great respect on account of its association with the saint's well. St. Begley's holy well is near the graveyard of Tulach a Begley. *Turas Fionnáin* in Oirear Dhumhaigh near Falcarragh, is made at a holy well on the very edge of the sea. A fountain of fresh water flows from the very rock. Here stations were made every quarter of the year, and on the 15th of August pilgrims prayed ten times around the well. It is said that St. Colmcille caused the water to flow from this rock to quench the thirst of St. Fionnán. It is named *Eas Fhionnáin* which means Fionnán's Fall (Waterfall). About a mile from Massinass school there is another Colmcille Well; stations, I gather, are still made there, and halfway between Creeslough and Dunfanaghy there is another Colmcille well at Kildarragh on the shore of Lough Colmcille. It is understood that older people and some of the young still make the *turas* there on the saint's feast day, June 9th. A cairn of stones on the hill above the well remains to indicate the numbers who have made the station down the ages. The little hill is called Cnoc a' Chuilinn. Strange to say that no fish have ever been found in Lough Colmcille, as it is related that the saint gave its water a left-hand blessing, because a fisherman had denied that he had caught fish and had lied. The same story goes for the beautiful Mulroy Bay. On the top of Kerrykeel Hill there is a holy well which is four miles to the east of Falcarragh and to which people still go and pray.

A VISIT TO GWEEDORE

A few visits should be arranged for Gweedore to see all that is worth seeing there. Indeed, there are many ways which the traveller might take and so become acquainted with those Green Glens of Gweedore, for as Patrick Mac Gill said: 'From the start you're striven and striving still, what road runs straight to the top of the hill.' Crolly Bridge can be crossed, and nearby the factory of those famous dolls of the same name can be visited. We can see the new industrial estate at Derrybeg, where there is good employment for workers whose forebearers in times gone by had no other prospect but the emigrant ship. About 1878 or 1879 a Mrs. Ernest Harte started an institution for teaching the peasants to use native dyes, such as heather, lichen, berries, soot and crotal from rocks, which were readily available, and their application to the wool and homespun yarn gave woven and knitted garments a decorative and pleasing appearance. Many are the changes since those enthusiastic efforts of that great woman, Mrs. Harte. There are now several firms like that of the I.D.A., Them, Radiators for export, G.T. Carpets, Europlast, Comer Yarns and Fibres, Telectron and a crisp factory, and great work has been accomplished by Gaeltarra Eireann, Radio na Gaeltachta and Anco Training Centres.

We can see Mullaghderg on the coast, where one of the ships of the Armada rests deep in the sands. About one hundred and forty years ago a man staying in the Rosses got as far as reaching the sunken vessel. A strong east wind and a spring tide had swept the sea out so far that the vessel could be seen. Later the same man and friends went by boat and found the ship visible from stem to stern. One of his friends sawed off a piece of the wood and planed it, and found it to be Spanish chestnut. On another occasion coast guard men with a crane fitted on two boats tried to lift a gun from the ship, but the tackle broke, and before the next tide a heavy storm had arisen and nothing since has been heard or seen of the sunken Spanish ship of the Armada.

LORD GEORGE HILL

Landlords in nineteenth century Ireland were not men to be respected. This was especially true in north-west Donegal. One famous Donegal landlord was Lord George Hill who purchased 23,000 acres of land in Tullaghbegley, Gweedore about 130 years ago. There are many stories told about this man which make him out to be an honest and progressive landlord on the one hand while on the other hand he seems to have done more to blacken the name of the poor people of Gweedore than all the landlords of Ireland could. The main controversy concerning Lord George Hill concerns his ideas of abolishing the old system of land division — the rundale system. Under this system land was let not in small farms or in compact squares, but in shares in so many fields. The good will or tenant right was transmitted by gift, sale or will, and infinitely sub-divided. Lord Hill tells of an instance where a field of half an acre had twenty-six holdings in it, and he also knew of a man whose small farm existed in thirty-two separate pieces.

THE RUNDALE SYSTEM

The system of letting, dividing or selling, not by the acre, but by the 'cow's-grass' was so complicated that a man would leave to his son one cow's-grass in a certain field — the extent of ground being fixed by its quality. There was a further sub-division into fourths of a 'cow's-grass', each known as one 'cow's foot', and one eighth of a 'cow's grass' which was known as 'one cleet' or half a foot. The result was, as the old saying goes — 'everybody's business was nobody's business'. Nobody would manure the land for his neighbour's benefit, nobody would sow turnips or clover grass for his neighbour's sheep to eat, so agriculture was reduced to mere rudimentary operations, and there were endless disputes. The rundale arrangement without a doubt must have dated back to the time when all land was the common heritage of a sept or clan. Often this old joint arrangement extended itself to animals — a horse was often jointly owned by as many as three or four small farmers or land holders. A story has been told of a poor horse which was jointly owned by three men on one of the islands. The horse went lame because none of the three would pay for shoeing more than one foot, each kept one foot in order, but the fourth went unshod. If a man reclaimed some mountain land, he was allowed only one crop of it, and afterwards it would be divided among the tenants of the townland in proportion to the rent each paid. To change this Lord Hill explained his project to an unwilling people who were slow for change, and rather suspicious of anything good coming from a landlord. However, he suggested a committee of tenants to assist — no man would be dispossessed, no man would be robbed of his tenant right. A system of fencing was arranged and premiums were offered for the best kept cottages, for the best field of turnips, for good fencing and gradually new habits were adopted by the people.

It may now be worthwhile to compare the standard of living with those years in the 1830s, when that critical writer Carlyle visited Gweedore and was met at Letterkenny by Lord George Hill. They drove by side-car from Letterkenny to Ballyarr, through Kilmacrenan, over Harrow Bridge and on between Dooish and Errigal, and Carlyle commenting said — 'I never rode or walked or drove in any region such a black dismal twenty-two miles of road in any country'. No such comments in the 1970's when there are many fine and modern houses. People may still have complaints, but the standard of living is tolerable in comparison with those times. In describing his host, Carlyle left us a description of a kindly nobleman: 'He is handsome, grave, a smiling man of fifty or more; thick grizzled hair, elegant club nose, low cooing voice, military composure and absence of loquacity. A man you love at first sight'. And, after his sojourn to that part of county Donegal, Carlyle again praised his host saying 'In all of Ireland, lately in any other land, saw no such beautiful soul'. Other writers may have used different words. No one cares to leave Gweedore in a hurry now, and our travellers will feel equally slow to part from such affectionate people. Even though we have covered much ground there, no one would care to go without first learning a little of those much spoken of days of evictions.

THE GWEEDORE EVICTIONS

In February, 1889, the whole Gweedore district was in a state of war, one might call it. The Plan of Campaign had been begun and great evictions followed on the Olphert estate. Troops were sent, and brought with them the much talked of 'Battering Ram' which they used for knocking down those mountain homes, whose inmates refused to open their doors to officers of the law. The feelings of the people were running high, and their leader was the priest, Father James MacFadden, who in all meetings and discussions with the landlords and the forces, acted as their spokesman. He was held in the highest degree and much respected by his flock, and he was a man of strong character.

'Not long ago when rain and snow was blowing from
    the west,
Balfore's men rode down the glen, brave men for to arrest,
The Plan Campaign they did proclaim along the Fanad
    shore,
Took MacFadden bright the star and light from lovely
    green Gweedore.'

On Sunday, February 2nd, 1889, Father James was celebrating mass in the chapel, never thinking that the authorities would risk so unpopular a measure as his arrest. To the east of the old church a path leads up a steep incline to the priest's house, and during mass-time Inspector Martin and eight men were sent from Derrybeg school-house to take up positions on the priest's private path. Father James came out of the chapel still robed in the vestments, which he wore saying mass, and he was there and then arrested by Inspector Martin, and he demanded to see the warrant. The congregation of peasants gathered round and when the sergeant tried to force the priest up the hill, the men-folk became raged and with stakes and paling poles pulled from the ditches, they attacked the police. The inspector was separated from his men, with the sergeant and Father MacFadden in front of him. While the inspector managed for a while to keep the crowd off with his sword, he now ordered his men to fire. The crowd gathered in on the forces and held them and Inspector Martin lost his revolver. The whole attack passed so quickly that the force at the school-house didn't even know what was happening. Stones, sticks, and poles were flying and the inspector, making a movement, was struck down. Father MacFadden's sister and housekeeper went to open the door to let the priest in, but she was herself shut outside where she saw the Inspector battered to death. The crowd drew back from the body when Father MacFadden shouted to them from the window, but by then the inspector was dead. The priest was prosecuted for murder, but was acquitted. The weapons were paling stakes — not black-thorns, and no one would suppose that either priest or people contemplated such a bloody tragedy. Much blame was laid on the heads of the police officers, who entirely ignored not only the fierce temper of people enraged by a struggle for their homes, but also their extreme anger at what to them was a profanity. One of the sergeants was also beaten almost to death, and two men received a long imprisonment. Terrible though all this was there were no motives of private malignity and indeed the people who killed Inspector Martin would neither have robbed nor harmed a man or woman if they had met them alone and unprotected on their lonely hills. From ordinary crime Gweedore has been singularly free, and its people are held in the highest esteem, and have never dishonoured the county to which they belong.

'Brave Father James that hero's name, its him we do bewail,
For in a cell they guard him well in Derry's city gaol.
May the God of love who rules above on him his blessings pour,
For on that same soil our forefathers toiled in lovely green Gweedore.'

THE BIG FLOOD

Before leaving Gweedore a run down to Bunbeg and Derrybeg would be well worthwhile. On the south is the Clady River, with its succession of delightful swirling streams and pools. The harbour of Bunbeg is distinctively lovely; a little lake of salt water shut in by high rocks and entered by the narrowest cleft that it would seem possible to get a good sized vessel through it. Then, leaving Bunbeg travel eastward along the coast to Derrybeg for about two miles where there are still some of those old, whitewashed, good-natured thatched homes. At the foot of the hill a tiny stream flows under a bridge and in the little hollow is Derrybeg chapel. In this hollow during the time of the penal laws, the people of the district gathered to hear mass in the open air. It was a well hidden hollow, and sentries posted in the high heather could easily guard the celebrant against a surprise visit by the Redcoats. In later times when those penal laws were repealed, and Derrybeg was in a position to build a new church, the people were determined that the new chapel should be built on this same spot of memories. The chapel was actually built across the little stream, and one Sunday morning in the early eighties a heavy flood came down and burst the culvert under the chapel instantly filling the building, and several people awaiting in the church were drowned.

DUNFANAGHY, HORN HEAD, MACSWINEY'S GUN

We can visit Dunfanaghy a neat clean little town sited on one of the most beautiful loughs or inlets of ocean that indent the whole northern coast of Donegal. Here at Dunfanaghy travellers should stop a day or two, and Horn Head can be visited where viewing those cliffs from a boat is a sight to remember, as they rise 600 feet and best viewing is from the sea. The millions of sea-birds that build there and live there in all seasons are a sight on their own. Many years ago a watcher who protected nets which were set for salmon had a narrow escape from death. Seals follow salmon right into the nets, and with their sharp teeth they can cut the nets, so if a seal's head is seen bobbing over water, a bullet from a gun is usually on its way towards it. This watcher came near to a tragic end for himself and his son. He had taken his boy with him for company, but rough stormy weather came, and no boats could get near his landing place. His food supply ran out, and he could not communicate with anyone or any place. The cliff above him could be climbed, though few have ever tried to scale it. However, the watcher seeing there was no other way out, tied the boy on his back and began climbing from ledge to ledge to reach the top, three hundred feet above. They safely made it, but strange to say, tragedy struck both man and boy within a short space of time. The boy fell over the same cliff while trying to come on a cormorant's nest, and the father on his way home across the moor fell while jumping over a small ditch, and was found with his neck broken.

While on this excursion we can view the ring of cliffs extending westward from the Horn, where they gradually get lower and decrease in height to around one hundred feet. The historical MacSwiney's Gun can be visited, where a cave runs in from the sea, and from the end of the cave a chimney-like hole rises to the cliff top. In a storm the wave is forced into the opening and is shot out through the narrow chimney in a straight jet. This powerful body of water carries with it heavy stones, and in this narrow chamber there is an explosion like that of a cannon gun. At times they say it can be heard in Derry, and also at Ards which is seven or eight miles away. The MacSwiney who was owner in times long ago, had his headquarters in Doe Castle, a little beyond the Gun.

Our centre at Gartan still stands good for the purpose of our outings and excursions. From here we can spend days in those lovely spots made famous by our own Bridie Gallagher's songs – The Girl from Donegal. It was here in Creeslough that Bridie first saw the light, and in the late 1940's and 1950's she took the world by storm with those songs of the hills. Many ballad groups have come and gone since those early days when the girl from Donegal gave new life to Irish ballads. It was herself who was such a great ambassador and who enchanted crowded theatres in many lands and won many hearts to love and learn the songs of our land. We can hardly leave her loved village without looking around to see if they're 'Cutting the corn in Creeslough the day'.

CREESLOUGH AND BEYOND

As we make our way from Creeslough to Ards there are many attractive views from every turn of the road. Looking towards the coast we can see on one of the inlets of Sheephaven Bay, Ards House, surrounded with beautiful woods, a most desirable place to call, where the sons of St. Francis now care, pray and work that extensive and beautiful demesne. English soldiers of fortune who served Her Majesty, Queen Elizabeth, in her wars with the O'Donnells received rewards of land from this portion of the Ulster chieftain's territory. In 1603 John Wray took possession of Ards, which passed right down through Henry Wray and his wife, sister of Lord Arran. They later moved to Letterkenny. Their second son Humphrey was the father of the well known William Wray, Master of Ards. He married the sister of Sir Henry Hamilton, and was connected in one way or another with nearly all the planted families of the time in Donegal and the neighbouring counties. At his mansion he feasted high, and invited the high and mighty from afar. It was said of him that the home of the Master of Ards 'snowed with meat and drink', and his oxen were sent across the mountain passes to meet his guests and help to carry their gifts and equipment.

Our modern methods of transport have made the carrying of such booty much less cumbersome, so with more ease we can accomplish that visit to Ards and to the Franciscans. On our coastal trip around deep Sheephaven Bay we can visit Rosapenna and Downings Bay, and their beauty on a fine day has to be seen to be believed. The cyclist or hiker should see and follow the Bunlin river which leads you along an exciting and romantic course right down to Mulroy Bay, showing a very fine cascade at the Golden Loop. The Mulroy with its shores of coastline can best be seen along its western shore between Carrigart and Milford. On its eastern shore lies the extensive district of Fanad with its long history back through the O'Breslins, descendants of Connaing, third son of Conall Gulban, son of the first High King of Ireland, who possessed Tyrconnell. The O'Breslins were followed by the MacSwynes who became established there and built several fortresses. Fanad is set between short ranges of hills running across the peninsula. The Knockalla hills rise to a height above the sea of 1,200 feet. A winding road across them has become one of the wonders of modern times for its wonderful scenery and beauty. It was a big job of work helped and encouraged by the well known Donegal politican Neil Blaney who foresaw what its beauty would mean to the visitor and stranger. So much regard was given to Neil's judgement in this project, that locally this road across the cliffs is known as 'The Blaney Road'. A number of loughs are on the way or nearby, between Milford and Ramelton and fresh-water fishing is in plenty. The names of some of these inland lakes are Nakey lake, The Bog Lough, Aweel, Maheradrummond, Thorn Lough, Green Lough and Glencarn. To the north east of Milford we can fish in the waters of Milford Lough, Uifinn, Columcille, Coney and Doo and good brown trout can be caught in the waters of most of those lakes.

THE LORD LEITRIM MURDER

To the western side of Milford the traveller comes to a
shadowed wood on Mulroy's shore, and here at Cratloe the
murder of the hard-headed Earl of Leitrim was executed. It
was nine o'clock on the morning of the 2nd of April, 1878,
as the Lord drove with his servant and clerk from Manor
Vaughan, and at the entrance to this wooded stretch of
road he encountered this early morning shock. There are
various views of this murder of Lord Leitrim, of the persons
involved and the plans which were made, but one thing is
certain – the master of Manor Vaughan was not a loved
landlord amongst the peasantry of Fanad and districts. It
is now one hundred years ago since this murder took place,
but around the shores of Mulroy Bay it is spoken of as if it
happened quite recently.

In 1960 there was a celtic cross erected and a booklet
published to the memory of the Fanad Patriots. It may still
be possible to procure a copy which tells much about those
sad happenings. The third Earl of Leitrim had served in the
British Army and many people speak of him as a man by no
means bad, and who possessed some good qualities. He was
not one of the absentee landlords who has been a real curse
on our land. The care of his property was the main occupation of his life, and he always travelled armed. He did abolish
the old system of rundale, while other landlords allowed it
to drag on in all its setbacks. However, the aims of the 1870
act which gave the tenant an interest in his holding was in
no way favoured by Lord Leitrim. No opposition was allowed
to stand in his way. If one man sold his tenant-right to
another, the Lord would simply evict both. He had a violent
temper and to his tenants he was, in plain English, a tyrant.
He was not an avaricious landlord, as his rents were not un-
usually exorbitant; but he insisted that every holding on his
estate should be held absolutely at his landlord's pleasure.
He did not approve of a tenant making improvements even
at his own cost, and in such cases he either raised the rent,

97

or evicted the tenant to establish his authority. With a capricious temper, and violent prejudices it is easy to see how injustices were carried out.

Eviction in those out of the way places and in those times meant a denial of the only means of livelihood. When asked by a clergyman of the parish for help for a family which had been evicted, Leitrim's reply was 'Sir, I would not give you a blanket to cover their bones'. The tenantry tensed and smarting under such 'laws of the lash' had come to the end of their patience. At the entrance to Cartlagh Wood on Mulroy's shore the Third Earl of Leitrim was to receive his first command from the tenants; to prepare for instant death. As Lord Leitrim always kept his gun at the ready, it had been thought strange that he did not reply to the ring-leader by a discharge of arms; but his defensive weapons was this time not at hand, and in a matter of seconds the old Lord with his grey hairs blowing in the wind was pulled from his coach and done to death and his body flung into the ditch. Lord Leitrim was in his seventy third year. The place selected was well thought out, the timing of his journey was almost perfect, all circumstances seemed to favour his attackers, and the murderers of the Lord of Manor Vaughan escaped by boat. Having earlier come up the Mulroy with a fair wind and an incoming tide, they tied their boat in a dark recess where it could not be seen. His serfs around, near and far, raised noises of condemnation of Lord Leitrim's treatment. Throughout his estates as well as in the neighbouring districts there were feelings of relief on his removal. The Lord of the Manor evidently pushed his notion of "landlord's rights" beyond his tenants' endurance. What the real cause of this resolute murder was no one has clearly expressed, but it has been said that eighty processes of ejectment were pending when his life was taken, and that there was then no question of a con-spiracy to deny him his rent.

It was a hired car that the Earl used as he set out from Manor Vaughan to drive to Milford; beside the driver, was his clerk, a young boy of twenty-five years, who was but a short time in his service. Behind them was another hired car in which was Lord Leitrim's confidential servant; but the horse in this car became lame and in a short space of time was left about a mile behind. The second car had almost reached the place where Cartlagh wood divides the road from Mulroy when they heard two shots fired. When they got over the brow of the hill, they saw in front of them at some distance the car with only Lord Leitrim on it. Then they could see him struggling with two men; the account does not give much detail of the struggle, but it is apparent that they made no great haste to come to the spot. The clerk came running towards them, saying the driver was shot. Their horse, frightened at a black lump on the road, refused to pass it. The lump was the body of the driver of the first car. Then they came to Lord Leitrim lying in a shough with his brains beaten out. Meanwhile two men were pulling out from the lough shore and rowing away, and in no time were lost from view behind one of Mulroy Bay's many islets. The clerk died as they stood there, though the only wound they could see was one made by a slug above his ear. It was felt he had died from a violent shock rather than from the wound. The driver of Lord Leitrim had his heart riddled with shots, but the Lord had no fatal shot-wound, he was done to death with gun butts. The plan was well made and cleverly carried out, the timing was to the dot. Yet its success was surprising, for there was a patrol of two policemen on the same road, within half a mile who met the frightened horse galloping down to Milford by itself. At this particular point of the road where the assassination took place, the road comes to within fifty yards of the water's edge. Here there is a slope from the road down, thickly covered with wooding and shrubbery, so it was easy to hide the boat, while the assailants had but to keep under cover and await the sound of Lord Leitrim's trotting horses.

The driver was the first killed with the first shots and the clerk dropped off; seemingly the car went on a little further, but was stopped as Lord Leitrim jumped off to struggle with the two men. He was known to be a tough man and, with his teeth hard set, he had died in a life or death struggle. The boat was found on the far side of Mulroy, with the oars in her. A rough, broken gun butt, a pistol and a gun were found at the scene of the murder. The question asked afterwards was, why Lord Leitrim had not his revolvers that day in the car he was riding on, but left them in the accompanying car unloaded? The answer has never come forth, yet it could be that the reason was well known.

Four men were tried for the murder on circumstantial evidence; a torn page of copybook found, was fitted to a torn page in a book in one of their homes. One died in jail before the trial; the remaining three were acquitted, but died within a year or two. Around that countryside it was maintained that the chief man in the affair lived for many a year after, but travel a five miles radius around Milford, and many of the natives, could, but would not, tell you who it was that killed the Lord of Manor Vaughan.

THE NEW EARL

The oppressive system practised by Lord Leitrim was much changed when the Earl's nephew and successor, who was an officer in the British navy, took over Manor Vaughan. He came at once to the scene of the murder, and became conspicuous by his attempts to bring the criminals to justice. Nevertheless, he rode around the country unguarded. The tenants soon became aware that the new boss of Manor Vaughan had learned from errors, and from previous mistakes and common-sense called him to apply a new order and more concern for those not-so-well-off tenants on Leitrim estates. He first set about reinstating all those who were listed for ejectment by his uncle. His greatest undertaking and contribution to that whole countryside was his setting up of a line of steamers to carry the produce of farms to Glasgow, and bring back materials and articles in demand, to Milford. By this service of transport he enabled local shop-keepers to take almost a pound-a-ton from their charges, which would have to be paid in freight to transport goods from Derry Quay. Such changes and improvements in and around the Mulroy restored a good name to Manor Vaughan, and raised Milford from a struggling village to one of the most thriving towns in county Donegal. But true to the proverb – 'the good die young' – this well thought of and enlightened Earl was prematurely called from this world, from a people he learned to love and regard and from the numerous projects which he financed to help them. The sorrow of his early death was expressed in many a humble home and with sad and tender feelings of sorrow, a vast throng of people and priests followed his funeral to a quiet little cemetery at Carrigart.

THE ROSAPENNA AND PORTSALON HOTELS

In moving off from Cratloe Wood and from its shady oak and hazel trees, we may catch a glimpse of that once well-cared-for Melmore pier which was built by the young Lord Leitrim at his own expense to change the water of the Mulroy into a shipping course of commerce. This shipping service convenienced travellers to and from Glasgow and Derry, as well as locals seeking employment, or going to or from those places. It was also a boon to the Rosapenna and Portsalon hotels as tourists could disembark at the pier beside Mulroy House. Both those fine hotels are well known ever since those far off days, for the fine service they have given and the keen golfer has that added attraction of having the golf links outside the doors of Portsalon and one of the finest courses in Ireland. There is no need for me to try to describe them. Local tourist pamphlets will give all the information required for any amount of golf and plenty of pleasant hours of fishing and all these great centres are fully licensed.

From Portsalon we can look across Lough Swilly and Ballymastocker with its bright sands and to the right the sandhills and behind them the pleasant green of the golf links. Facing you is Dunree Head and you will get the fullest view of Lough Swilly by crossing to the Inishowen side where it can be seen to slant or curve somewhat eastward and then turn south. From a good vantage point you will see clearly its open waters for about ten to fifteen miles. Away to the left of Portsalon you see a range of cliffs or rugged spinks for about six miles out to Fanad Head, reaching to a square-set cliff called the Bin of Fanad, with a fall of around three hundred feet.

KILMACRENAN

For another excursion let us set out from Gartan in the south eastern direction and make our way to Kilmacrenan or Cill Mhac nÉanáin which is a place revered as the foster-home of St. Columba who founded an abbey there. It was here at Kilmacrenan that the saint's brother-in-law and lord of the territory lived. Around this town or village called after the name of its benefactor, Éanán, there grew up another Franciscan Priory, but later a Protestant parish church was built there. Little is left of St. Columba's own venerable abbey except a small slender tower with a few pointed windows. The old spot is situated in a remarkable highland valley, where its beauty is added to by a fresh, clear rushing river.

A short distance from Kilmacrenan we come to the Rock of Doon, where the chieftains of the O'Donnell's were invested. These traditional ceremonies were of a very sacred nature and it is thought that they were partly performed at the abbey and partly at this historic Rock of Doon. A description of what took place is left by Lynch, who seems to have been well informed. He says:

"When the investiture of the O'Donnell took place at Cel-Mhac-Crenain, he was attended by O'Ferghail, successor to Columbkille and O'Gallachuis, his Marshal and surrounded by the Estates of the country. The Abbot O'Ferghail put a pure white straight unknotted rod into his hand and said, 'Receive Sire, the auspicious ensign of your dignity, and remember to imitate in your government the whiteness, straightness and unknottiness of this rod, to the end that no evil tongue may find cause to asperse the candour of your actions with blackness, nor any kind of corruption, or tie of friendship be able to prevent your justice. Therefore, in a lucky hour take the government of this people, to exercise the power given to you with freedom and security'. The proud recipient of this religious ceremonial, while taking the oath to maintain the laws and privileges of his ancient realm, was placed in the footprints of the first Chieftain."

According to the Four Masters these were cut into the inauguration stone which was kept in the abbey. Dr. O'Donovan in his notes at the Royal Irish Academy mentions the belief that this much sought after stone which has long since disappeared may still be in the possession of the family of an unknown thief.

DOON WELL

In the same district and on the same day we can easily call to that holy well so well known throughout the whole county of Donegal — Doon Well. Here, from time unending, rich and poor have knelt to pray at this well. Just beyond it is a bank where pilgrims take off their footwear and wash their feet in the little stream, as a sign of clean and pure intentions, and sincerity of approach for the cure of ailments. Then say five Our Fathers and five Hail Marys and one Creed, and drink from its waters praying to God to speed you in the errand which brought you here. Then say five more Our Fathers and five Hail Marys for the bottle of water you take away; then one for Father Friel, the priest who blessed the well, and one for Father Gallagher the curate, and an Our Father and Hail Mary for the man who put the covering stones on the well, that his soul will have peace for his good deed.

It is well I remember the preparations in my own district when a party of friends and neighbours were getting ready for a penitential visit to this place of pilgrimage. By side-cars and train they travelled through Barnesmore Gap and there is still one old man alive who walked with his uncle over forty miles across the mountains in his bare feet. It was the view, in those times, that only by prayer and penance were you sure of reaching the kingdom of Heaven. In those times also there was strong faith in the healing

103

powers of the waters from this well and bottles of Doon Well water found its way around the world. The numbers of pilgrims who have visited the well down the years can be gauged to some extent by the votive offerings and reminders of pain and infirmities left there. The crutches, sticks, the medals and strings of beads that wind, sun and rain have bleached into the same grey colouring of the stones around them — they all help to tell the story of Doon Well. Many a person has made the Doon Well *turas* and prayed the stations for the cures and needs of others. One old woman travelled on foot six miles, and a visitor passing wished her quick relief from her illness. 'Oh, thanks be to God', said she, 'there's nothing the matter with me, but my son in Scotland says there's a lot of illness around where he lives, and that an amount of people are ill, so I thought I should come to the well and pray for them'. She carried with her a bottle of Doon Well water which you could be sure found its way to her son in Scotland. She was cheerfully on her way home, over the six miles she had already travelled to the well, happy to have done what she thought was best for those suffering and who were far from this holy well. What she had, she gave freely of — the holy water, her prayers and a twelve mile walk on a warm summer's day. God would hardly let such generosity pass unnoticed.

ST. COLMCILLE

Before leaving St. Colmcille's birthplace, Gartan, and his foster home Kilmacrenan with its nearby Doon Well beloved in history, let us note just a few points in the life of that saint from Donegal and from Ireland. To this very time Donegal people feel a sense of pride to be able to claim Saint Colmcille as one of their own, and his name is revered all over the length and breadth of the county. His name is given to one of its parishes and throughout the county are scattered relics and traditions of his life and works. Born in 521 A.D. he was, according to custom of the time, placed in fosterage with relatives at Kilmacrenan and as Adamnán, who wrote the saint's life, says:

'He was instructed in the love of Christ, and by the grace of God, and his zeal for wisdom had so preserved the integrity of his body, and the purity of his soul, that though dwelling on earth he appeared to live like the saints in heaven'.

When the time came for serious studies, he moved from his foster home and joined the school of St. Finian, and made a course of studies under this famous teacher at Strangford Lough. From St. Finian's school he moved to Clonard and in order of time went to other seats of learning like St. Mobhí's, Glasnevin where holiness and science went hand in hand. After his ordination and taking of holy orders, he walked the length and breadth of Tyrconnell leaving his monuments of piety and zeal from Derry to Tory, on hill and island, on cliffs, by rugged coasts and in the silence of deep glens.

His blessings went far beyond the bounds of Tyrconnell; his holiness and his miracles marked him out as a man of God, and disciples flocked to his fold. He founded many abbeys including Derry, Durrow, Swords and Kells, all of them renowned in ecclesiastical teaching. In his forty-second year (563 A.D.) St. Colmcille took to missionary work and sailed from Ireland to Scotland to teach the pagans, as they were in those days, to the love of Christ. In Scotland he was welcomed by Conall, King of the Albanian Scots who was related to him, and gave him the island of Hy or later known as Iona. Twelve disciples accompanied him and helped him to lay the foundations of the monastery of Hy which soon became the most famous in Northern Europe, and a recognised fountain of holiness and learning for centuries after. He planted the Cross of Christ from the Orkney Isles, in the Hebrides and south beyond the mountains to the Lowlands and into Northumbria. He is said to have built three hundred houses to the service of God, and to have written as many manuscript books some of which survive to the present day.

St. Colmcille died in his seventy sixth year. He was buried in Iona, but his bones were afterwards taken to Downpatrick where they were placed in the same tomb with those of St. Patrick and St. Brigid.

The Tired Crane

A very touching but beautiful story is told of the Saint's affection for his native home. It happened while Colmcille was in Iona. One day he called one of the brothers and said to him that a crane knocked about by storms and winds would land weary and fatigued, and lie down on the shore or beach of the island quite exhausted. 'Treat the bird with tenderness', said the Saint, 'take it to a neighbouring house where it can be nursed for a few days — three days and three nights. When it has recovered and is refreshed, after that time it will fly back directly to its home in Ireland. I am anxious about the bird because it comes from my own native place'. The good brother did as he was told, the bird came and after careful nursing for three days, it took wing gently, rising to a great height and making its path through the air, directed its course across the sea to Ireland as straight as it could fly on a calm day.

ON TO RATHMULLAN

Along the central reach of Lough Swilly from Macammish to Buncrana, from Fahan all around Rathmullan, some very ancient traces of past history can be seen. At Buncrana there is an old castle of the O'Dohertys', and another can be seen on Inch Island. Further south, overlooking the arm of the lough that runs towards Letterkenny, Burt Castle stands on a hill top. But from Fahan pier or from Lough Swilly itself a monument of a much older past is still on view. On the highest hill of the range that divides the eastern arm of Lough Swilly from the valley of the Foyle and Derry, on that top of Elagh mountain, stands a circular fort of stone, that is Grianán or Sunny Chamber, summer palace of Aileach, and the visitor should see this ancient building — a place of wonder.

Three ramparts of earth and stone enclose a fort or cashel, a ring of masonry some twenty five yards in diameter, with walls eighteen feet high and over twelve feet thick at the base. Inside galleries run from the gates and exit on to the enclosure. It is said that it was here that the sons of Niall of the nine Hostages established themselves.

As we approach the neat little town of Rathmullan, the stranger will be attracted by the pleasant range of hills at its back, the highest point of which is Cnoc an Aifrinn (The height or hill of the Mass). A walk to the top would give a few hours of good viewing and much pleasure to the hiker or hill climber. The ruins of a Carmelite priory are in the town and a castle nearby was once occupied by the McSwiney Fanad.

It is not the castle at Rathmullan with its various styles of architecture, nor yet the ruins of the holy priory, that keep Rathmullan so much to the forefront of Tyrconnell's history. Of more importance was the town's vivid witnessing of the end of the chieftain's of the North and the intrigue which led to that end as it was from here that the Earls of Tyrone and Tyrconnell and many of their relations fled in 1607. This 'Flight of the Earls' led to the plantation of Ulster with Scottish and English colonists on the vast estates of land left by the Earls and which were subsequently confiscated.

ALONG LOUGH SWILLY'S SHORE

Before leaving Rathmullan and Lough Swilly, that centre which has kept us a while, with its 'in and outs and round abouts' so rich in history, let us have a relaxed view along the north western shore, heading for Letterkenny. This is a drive, hike or journey for the cyclist, beautiful beyond compare. The view of the Swilly and its coasts are exciting, and there are many fine places to see if time is kind. There are famous and ancient homesteads like Castlegrove, Castle Wray and Barnhill. Beyond the well-known Ardrumman House we can see ruins of Killydonnell Abbey, a Franciscan monastery of the sixteenth century. The landscape views from this old O'Donnell foundations are beautiful, with land and sea of the purest blue and a coast of green to the water's edge. There is a mixture of waving wooded valleys and beautiful residences sloping towards the hills of Fanad and Inishowen. There is a legend about the Bell of Killydonnell, which relates that when it was taken by traders or marauders from Tyrone who ransacked the abbey it was loaded into a waiting ship along with many other valuables. After the vessel moved out to cross the Swilly a violent storm arose, and the sacrilegious robbers with all their illbegotten goods, including the abbey bell, never reached the Tyrone side, but sank to the bottom of the lake. The story ends by saying that once every seven years the muffled tones of Killydonnell's bell are heard at the silent hour of midnight from that lake of shadows.

HOLY WELLS IN NORTH DONEGAL

At Inishowen — near Grianán of Aileach, can be found Tobar Phádraig or St. Patrick's Well, in the townland of Carrowrea. It is on the south-western side of Greenan Hill, and close by the historic Grianán of Aileach Castle which we talked about on our way to Rathmullan. The well is shallow, irregularly shaped and at present it has unsightly mossy growths bordering its edges. It is said to have been blessed by St. Patrick, but that it had been closed and forgotten until the last century when it was discovered and re-opened with religious ceremony by some priests from Derry city. It is told that not too long ago a local resident contaminated its waters, but soon after paid dearly for such an act. No fixed date appears to be observed for stations, but every Sunday during the summer months people from Derry pray beside the well, and drink of its water. Little shrubs around the well tell of those who came and cared, and left behind little memoirs. The Madman's Well at the Port a' Doruis is near Inishowen Head, and at Clonmany we have three holy wells.

Tobar Cholmcille or Colmchille's Well at Binnion

Local tradition has it that St. Patrick in company with

his sister and her two sons came to Clonmany. Both Chonais at the south of Binnion Hill was said to have been built by them. The holy well is in Binnion townland not far from the site of the ancient monastery. The tide passes over the well, but when it ebbs the water is still fresh. It is believed that if cattle were driven between the well and the shore at full tide, it would render them safe from disease. Its waters are also a cure for infertility. There is no *turas* now, but when it was done it started at the old church Straid, and there were five stations between the church and the holy well.

In the Gap of Mamore

This holy well in the Gap of Mamore, is said to have been dedicated to St. Eigne from whom Díseart Eigne got its name. On the 15th of August the *turas* is made. It is known as 'Turas Mhaidin Móir'. It is said that a saint of olden times retired to the silence of this mountain to meditate on the great Creator, and to supplicate His mercy and protection. It would seem to have been a very suitable place for such meditation and prayer.

St. Mura's Holy Well — Fahan

Saint Mura was a saint of the seventh century. His holy well is at Fahan and a *turas* is made there on 21st of March. St. Mura died 645 A.D. His crozier and chain are in the National Museum, Dublin. His chain is described as being seven feet five inches long, each link being made of a short piece of brown wire, the overlapped ends of which are flattened and rivetted together. Many miracles are spoken of as a result of *turas* to his holy well. The preservation of his well is accredited to a good-hearted native of Inishowen who did not share the religious beliefs of those pilgrims who came to pray there. Nevertheless, it was he who asked the Lough Swilly railway engineers to respect this holy spot in making a curvature of the line. A former owner of St. John's, Mayor Marshal, J. P. and the venerated parish priest of Fahan, the late Rev. Bernard McEdlowney, also deserve great credit for the saving of this Holy Well.

Holy Wells West of Ballyliffen

The well of Ó Muirgheasa – Tobar Mhuiris or St. Maurice's well is in the townland of Ardagh, just west of Ballyliffin Strand. It is hard to get to, and the making of stations is difficult for strangers. It is located on the bed of a small river and the water passes out in the form of a waterfall or little cascade. The well, it is thought, may have some connections with the Ó'Muirgheasa of Clonmany. Nearby are beds of Diarmuid and Colmcille. The station used to be made at the well on the 15th of August, but people were often seen making it at other times also. On Slieve Sneachta, can be found Tobar na Súl or Well of the Eyes. It is locally believed that the waters of this well possess curative properties when applied to the eyes. Some say that the well became a holy well when blessed by bishops. Others say that it was blessed by St. Patrick during his forty days in the mountain district, while a great church was being erected under his guidance. About a mile from Quigley's Point near the Three Trees is Tobar Phádraig, with an ancient graveyard about one hundred yards from it. This well still has its visitors at all seasons of the year.

A Holy Well at Maghernaul, Isle of Doagh

At Maghernaul can be found the holy well of St. Bríd which was frequented by pilgrims up to the 1900's. St. Patrick's Lake is not far from Malin Head, and *turas* was made here until recent times. There was no special day, but pilgrims went fasting and walking and praying around the lake three times, and the whole lake was regarded as being holy. Near the lake is Picture Hill, where the picture or form of a spotted horse and two monsters are seen on its eastern slope. It is said that St. Patrick banished these from the lake and killed them. Hence the

110

little lake is now free from terror and in a quiet peace.

St. Brendan's Holy Well

At Culdaff there is a holy well dedicated to St. Brendan. His feast day is locally kept on 22nd of July. The *turas* is made at the Leany a spot in the Culdaff river where St. Brendan used to moor his boat on returning from voyages to Scotland, as the tide fills up the river for a good way past its boundary. The Scottish coast can be seen from here on a clear day. Local tradition has it that the saint blessed the Port of Bunagee, at the mouth of the Culdaff river, and it is said that a fishing boat putting out from that port was never lost. So strong was this belief that new boats used to be brought overland from Malin and other places to be launched at Bunagee, so that they would have the benefit of St. Brendan's blessing. The present Protestant church of Culdaff occupies the site of St. Buadan's church, and the *turas* begins there. Prayers are said on three steps leading down to the Leany, which is not a well proper but a round pool in the river. A trough-shaped stone here is called St. Buadan's boat and St. Buadan's bell is kept in the parish in charge of the parish priest. It was a custom where cattle were bitten by a dog to drive them through the Leany at high tide. The animals were either cured, or got worse or indeed went completely mad on coming out of the water. An old man remembered such a case where the beast had to be shot immediately.

Devotions are performed at this holy well on any Friday all year round, and it is locally known that water taken from the Leany pool never grows stale when lifted with the recitation of a certain prayer. It is known that a person in the district had kept water from the Leany for 35 years and it was still as pure as when taken from the pool.

Holy Well at Malin Head

To the east of Gorman Church, called the 'Well Church' near Malin Head there is a holy well. It is covered at high

tide. A pattern is held there on 15th of August called
'Malin Well Fair', with tents and drinking, but no praying
is done. Older people say a *turas* was made on May Eve and
Mid-Summer Eve. It is said to have been blessed by a saint
of olden times and several cures which were very remarkable
are said to have been effected by the use of its waters for
healing sufferers. The remains of an old church are nearby.
Michael O'Clery in the Martyrology of Donegal under the
date, 3rd November, says: 'We find a Muirdealach, son of
Cuanna of the race of Irial. It is he that is called Muirdealach,
at the present day and in Inis Eoghain, his church and his
holiday are kept.' However, at the present day no one
remembers having ever seen a pilgrimage to this well on
this date. It wasn't an encouraging time of the year for
pilgrimage and it may well be that the 3rd of November
was never more than a church festival, but that with the
people, the observance of the *turas* was passed on as
being on May Eve and Midsummer Eve.

A *Turas* Between Carndonagh and Malin

Cathal Dubh's three boiling wells at Strabreagy are
three little bubbling springs on the Black Rock in Drumaville
townland, on the left of the road from Carndonagh to
Malin. At full tide they are covered, but there used to be
a *turas* there. Cathal Dubh was a hermit, and his cell is
still to be seen at Goorey just two miles from Malin on the
road to Lag.

A Holy Well at Moville

Near to Stroove, north of Moville and at the seaside
can be found a holy well, where stations are still made. It
was believed that Colmcille sailed from here to Iona.
There is a pillar-stone with an incised cross to mark the
spot. A very touching story goes with it, of how he sent
his boat down the Foyle, while he himself walked overland from Derry along the high western shore, so as to see
at intervals, or look back, at the high oaks of Derry which

he loved so dearly. As he reached Stroove, he could no longer see Doire (Derry, Doire – an oak grove) of his first foundations, so here in sadness he entered the boat for the Isle of Hy (Iona).

These few little lines show how dear Derry was to the great saint. They are from a poem said to have been written by himself:

'Come all Alba's cess to me
From its centre to its sea,
I would choose a better part;
One house set in Derry's heart.
Derry mine! my small oak grove,
Little cell, my home, my love!
O thou Lord of lasting life,
Woe to him who brings it strife.'

FROM RATHMULLAN TO LETTERKENNY AND THE HIRING

Taking a southward journey from Rathmullan we make our way towards Letterkenny. All along this drive we can notice very good land, and we can see those rich and fertile fields in the valley of the Lagan. This is a low flat river valley very rich in soil and famous for its yields of potatoes and flax. It is noted particularly for its production of good certified seed potatoes, which have a widespread market and a big export demand. The employment of servant boys and girls was a notable feature of this countryside. Most of these came from West Donegal, from Glenties, the Rosses, Dungloe and Gweedore; the mountain youngsters generally. It was at the 'Hiring Market' in Strabane which fell on the 12th of May that such hired contracts were made for the six summer months, and again on the 12th of November for the winter and spring months. This was a hard start to life in those days, which had practically ended about the middle of the 1930's. Towards the turn of the century the best wages a boy received was £5 for the six months, while a girl's wages would be around £3. The dialogue and customs of the hiring fair seemed strange to say the least, especially to the stranger. Groups of boys and girls would be arriving in the town of Strabane from an early hour, some after tramping upwards to forty miles, and perhaps after resting for some hours in a kindly inn, or some outhouse or animal's shelter. In lots of five and six you would notice them walk up and down the main street, while the keen-eyed farmer kept a watchful lookout for the manly lad or lassie whom he thought would best suit his farm requirements for the six month term ahead. Many of those young boys and girls were carrying their working clothes in bundles or parcels over their shoulders or under their arms. A farmer would then call the one of his choice from those groups as they paraded up and down, and present the youngster with many questions, while at the same time a circle of men and boys, perhaps ten to twelve, pressed around the two who stood face to face — the hirer and the hired. Many questions had already been put to the youngster by the prospective boss, questions relating to his farm experience; whether he was ever hired before; and if so his reason for not being re-employed. He would be asked about his knowledge of working with horses, about his ability to plough, sow, and mow, and if he were a good milker. He would be required to be available for milking and attending stock at least every second Sunday. Indeed many of the farmers of those days made sure you were at their service every Sunday, except while you attended your religious duties. This I know from my own personal experiences.

From now on most of the talking would be done by the onlookers, as they urged the boy; 'Speak up now don't be dumb with him. Get the best wages you can. Why wouldn't you? Say what's the least you'll take. But speak up'. Then there would be some low whispers between the boy and his friends, and the lad would return to the farmer and likely give an answer to an earlier question. 'When I go to it, I know what work is as well as any other man, and the work will be done as well as you would do it yourself, whether you are there or not. I know well, Mister, that you do be away a lot. I know you, though you may not know me'.

So the *colloguying* goes on. Now there's pause, and then a bystander, a friend perhaps of the lads asks them to come together. 'Say eight pounds ten now. Come now, John, you won't break my word'. He slaps the hand of young John, and tries to get the prospective boss to do the same, but no, nothing comes of it.

The onlookers now gather closer, they are anxious to see a bargain concluded, and the boss and the boy are taken by the shoulders. 'Come now. Off you go together and talk it out by yourselves. We don't want to hear what you are saying, its none of our business. Its you yourselves who will have to work together.' The two go off, and the immediate comment. 'He's asking eight pounds ten'. 'He's offered five'. 'Ah, but he's wanting eight pounds ten'. 'There was bigger boys in the market took less nor eight pounds'. 'Och, its not the size that counts; its the spirit. Them Ward lads were all good workers' 'Ah, an' he's a stout lad; no great size on him, but he's strong made'. The boy's points and make-up are discussed as if he were a draft-horse. The crowd gather around again and close in on the farmer and the farm-lad. All become part of the contract.

'Now John, no use in wrangling any longer. You say you'll take eight pounds. And, you Mister, say you'll give him five pounds'. 'Very well be dammit', says the farmer. Now an old man standing to the outside of the circle steps in. 'Here I'm listening to yous there this half hour. Give me your hand mister, whatever your name is. Here John, give me your hand, I'm making the price, I'm dividing the difference'. And, with the boys hand in the palm of the boss's hand, he claps the two with his own, and the boys wages for the six months farm work is made – six pounds ten shillings – and no money until the term ends. 'Good luck to you both'. It was only on the 12th of May or the 12th of November that the hiring fairs were held, but like many other customs of the past their days have ended, in that border town of Strabane, Co. Tyrone.

To the tourist whose interests are in the county Donegal scenery, Strabane, Co. Tyrone on the east border of Co. Donegal is of little interest, except as a starting point or

115

finishing stop, depending on which side of the county you enter. Letterkenny is a very convenient point from which to explore a very beautiful country of about a ten to twelve mile radius of the Cathedral town. It is a good centre for bus transport to any part of Co. Donegal, as well as for distant buses to Derry, Belfast or Dublin. Fishermen can enjoy very fine fishing in this location, particularly in the Lannan river where salmon and trout are obtainable. The Lannan river rises in Gartan Lough and flows into Lough Swilly at Ramelton. In parts it runs slowly and sluggish, while at other places there are some fine streams and broad deep pools, as well as nice gravelly shallows. It is a most enjoyable river to fish, as a twelve to fourteeen foot salmon rod would cover the greater part of it, and wading is not necessary. Salmon from seven to twenty five pounds in weight can be caught, the average size being from ten to thirteen pounds. There are lakes and tributary streams convenient to the Lannan river with very fine brown trout in plenty, and good catches can be made. The distances to various parts of the River Lannan from Letterkenny vary from five to twelve miles and a very grand circular tour can be made from it to principal villages, including Churchill, Conwal, Kilmacrenan and Milford. Cyclists will have good roads all around and there are very fine hotels and restaurants all over this location. Letterkenny has a handsome Catholic Cathedral which is a commanding feature for miles around. It stands on high ground overlooking a pleasant and thriving town of one large street facing east on the side of a hill. All the country around the town is a rich expanse of fertile lands, with neat, well-kept residences, and many colourful modern bungalows.

LET US GO TO RAPHOE

To cross eastward from Letterkenny, we go down the valley of the Swilly for a short distance, and turn to the right in a south-east direction, where we pass through a country not so scenic as to crave one to linger too long. Raphoe is eight and a half miles further east and sited near a great range of hills which slant down to decline in low-lands. Raphoe (Rath Bhoth — Ring-fort of the Huts) is a very old town. It was at one time rich and flourishing and gave its name to the diocese. St. Colmcille established a monastery here, which was later taken over by his great friend and relative Adamnan who enlarged and extended its structure.

Convoy is on the top of a hill about two miles from Raphoe and here at Beltanny there is a fine example of a stone circle consisting of sixty-seven stones and measuring about one hundred and fifty yards in circumference. The land towards the south and east of the town consists of many hillocks and generally dry land which lends itself to good cultivation. From Mullafin, 954 feet, you can look over the green undulating valleys of the Finn and the Deel rivers, while far beyond the Foyle the distant hills of Derry show in their glory. Nearer, the high mountain ranges of Donegal on all sides make for the skyline a majestic picture. Close by on the north-west is Cark mountain and near its top Lough Deel can be seen where the Burndale waters start their course, and flow south past Ballindrait to join the Foyle below Lifford. There is open country from Convoy through the neat village of Killygordan and as we head east, we arrive at the little town of Castlefinn situated near to the Tyrone border in the Finn Valley. Along the river Finn lies the boundary line between Tyrconnell and Tyrone. This demarcation line was fortified and ruled by the chieftains of Tyrconnell up to the beginning of the seventeenth century. Neil Garv lived here instead of in the Castle of Lifford which he claimed had been given to him by Hugh Dubh. He blamed Red Hugh for depriving him of this palace grandeur, and this grievance gave rise to such jealousy, which did not hesitate to bring about the betrayal of his fearless kinsman to the English, while at the same time placing himself at the service of the invaders.

TO COMPLETE THE CIRCUIT

For our travellers who have stayed with us all the way

between the Heather and the Sea from Lough Erne to Lough Swilly, and who would now like to complete the circuit back through Barnesmore Gap from the eastern side and on into Donegal town, we have a pleasant tour ahead. Taking the road at Castlefinn, we follow the river valley westward up to Stranorlar on this fine highway both for the motorist and the cyclist. It is now a busy thoroughfare and a changed road from those days when the Finn valley railway line was under consideration in 1860. At that time a survey was carried out in order to assess the amount of road traffic between Stranorlar and Strabane, and these were the figures which the observers came up with. In six days the following passed by: 12 vans, 909 carts, 275 jaunting cars, 14 gigs and horses, and 106 riders. All passengers conveyed numbered 1,105 for the six days. Well, those days of the dear old horse have gone and the motor-car now carries many more in a shorter time, but perhaps not with the same serenity or peace of mind.

The twin towns of Stranorlar and Ballybofey hold many memories of young days in those 1920's when the push-bike was all the rage around our mountains, and rich we thought ourselves if we were the proud owner of a bicycle. How often, when the spring sunshine had melted the snows of Croghconnellagh, we made our way, usually on Easter day, across beyond the Gap, as we used to say. We could be on our way to a dance in the Butt Hall which we seldom missed for an enjoyable night at Easter, or we could be making our way to that very obliging bicycle mechanic, Joe Rolston whom we could always approach, let it be Saturday or Sunday, and obtain the necessaries to keep our wheels going round, at his very reasonable prices. But no matter what mission we went on through the Gap, we never failed to pull up at that hospitable home of the Glacken family with their door and windows facing the east and looking across on Lough Mourne, always ready to welcome the travellers coming through the Gap. Many an enjoyable Sunday evening we spent in that same mountain home. The stretch of flattish mountain around Lough Mourne is most dreary and good only for turf, where there are some fine turf banks and the best of black turf can be harvested there. Lough Mourne is the source of the Mourne Beg river, which, flowing eastward courses on to unite its waters with the River Finn at Lifford. It would be well to remind our visitors that within the little cemetery attached to the Protestant parish church of Stranorlar the grave of Isaac Butt can be found and a prayer can be said for that great man of Home Rule who formed ideas which Stewart Parnell matured and carried forward afterwards. Isaac Butt, for the most part of his public life, was without doubt the great Irish orator of the English House of Commons as well as a noted figure of the Irish Bar. He received his first lessons at a Grammar School not far from his home town, Stranorlar, where he developed the great appetite for intellectual culture and eloquence which he later possessed.

In a letter to a very dear friend, Isaac Butt wrote from Dublin in 1867:

'If wherever I die, I would wish to be buried in Stranorlar churchyard. A very shallow grave would be enough, with a mound of earth or a tomb raised over it, as close as may be to the south-eastern angle. Put no inscription over the grave, except the date of my birth, and death; and wherever I am buried let the funeral be perfectly private, with as few persons attending, and as little show and expense as possible'.

So, the brilliant but humble lawyer and great Irishman had his wishes carried out and rests in his native soil in that sheltered and quiet churchyard by the Finn. Frances Brown, the well known blind poetess also came from Stranorlar, Co. Donegal.

If time permits we can drive or cycle the few miles from Stranorlar up along the river Finn where the road runs side by side with the river, and see the castle and great woods of Drumboe, where a quiet lonesome silence seems to cover this demesne, and recalls at least to the writer those sad times of fifty-eight years ago when on a March morning four Irish Republican soldiers were executed here in the grounds of this ancient castle. Three of them had come from County Kerry, and one from County Derry, all of them had been on the run around the Donegal mountains with many others, who like themselves never accepted a treaty with England which divided the six counties from the rest of Ireland, and split this small nation in two, an act which has never since lent itself to peace in this land.

As we prepare for our journey through Barnesmore Gap to the town of Donegal we can look forward to a very nice drive. However, many a one sighs for those days, when the narrow gauge-train or rail-bus brought us back home, as we would say, along this picturesque side-of-the-mountain line of wild and rugged scenery. What a nice three quarters of an hour ride it was. The joy of travelling, the homely atmosphere, the familiar accents and the arrival at the little station to meet the ones we loved.

DESTINATION DONEGAL

With our coastal and highland tourist circle of county Donegal completed, we can meet again on the Diamond, Donegal town. Looking south the Old Abbey can be reached on foot within minutes, and looking north the visitor can walk across in a few minutes to O'Donnell's Castle, where the clear waters of the river Eske flow by to meet the sea. Our tourists and visitors can be forgiven should their curiosity prompt them to enquire why the name of this northern region of Ireland changed, and when such a change took place. So often on our journeys into the history of this mountainous county we have used the beautiful name Tyrconnell and it seems a great shame to now have it as but a reminder of past history. Well, this change all began in the year 1584, when Sir John Perrott assumed the Deputy Lordship of Ireland. In the following year he assembled a parliament in Dublin, and, according to the Four Masters the list of Septs present on this occasion included the names of Hugh O'Neill in the first place, then Hugh O'Donnell, chief of Tyrconnell, with John Og O'Doherty, chief of Inishowen; Turlough O'Boyle, chief of Boylagh; Owen O'Gallagher, O'Donnell's marshal. The decree that Tyrconnell shall be henceforth the county of

Donegal (Dún na nGall – Fort of the stranger) was now passed, but resisted forcefully by the O'Donnell , who protested in the strongest manner against interference with the autonomy of Tyrconnell, and firmly declined to admit the English sheriff into his territory. But twenty two years later, after the Flight of the Earls, when the English had their own way, the name Tyrconnell became but a memory, and the name Donegal gradually came into general use.

THE FRANCISCANS IN DONEGAL

The memory of Neil Garv lingers long after his death in 1626, and many historians hold that, but for his treachery to Red Hugh, O'Donnell would have driven the English out of Donegal and Derry and most likely out of Ireland. After some years the Franciscan Friars who fled from the abbey in Donegal when they heard of Neil Garv's coming to take it, again gathered around the ruins of their former home. They sheltered in huts which they erected among the shattered walls and scattered rubble, and it was in these little shelters during the four years and six months between January 1632 and August 1636 that the chronicle known as the *Annals of the Four Masters* was written. This is an exhaustive account of the history of Ireland and was written by four great scholars of St. Francis' Order.

OUR LAST EXCURSION: ST. PATRICK'S PURGATORY

We would never be forgiven if we ended our guide of Donegal without at least an invitation to our visiting friends to come and share the deep satisfaction of making that station of penance and prayer, which has changed little since the middle of the fifth century, when its founder went across Tyrconnell on his first missionary journey.

Lough Derg is situated in the County of Donegal. The nearest town to it is Pettigo on the border between Donegal and Fermanagh. Lough Erne, which many claim as the most beautiful of Irish lakes, is but four miles distance from it. Bundoran too, situated on the Bay of Donegal is but a short journey. Lough Derg itself is a considerable volume of water and stands about 450 feet above sea level. The entire lake covers an area of 2,200 statute acres and measures about six miles in length, while its greatest width is a good four miles. It has 46 islands some of which are crowned with shady trees and shrubs, while some are bare to mountain storms. The names of these islands are strange and amusing: Inishgoose, Bilberry, Saint's Island, Friar's Island, Allingham's Island, Kelly's Island, Goat's Island, Derg Mor and Derg Beg, Trough Island and Bull's Island. There are other islands but unfortunately the names of these are now lost to us. Of its many islands two come in for special notice, namely Saint's Island, which is Lough Derg's largest and whereon stood the medieval Augustinian Monastery, and Station Island, the scene of the Pilgrimage known as St. Patrick's Purgatory.

St. Patrick's Purgatory, Lough Derg, is the oldest existing institution of the Irish Church. It links the days of St. Patrick with the present time. We are told from writings in a Louvain treatise of the 17th century, called the *Mirror of Penance*, how it was named St. Patrick's Purgatory. The saint having removed himself from the distractions of the world, went into a gloomy cave. There he prayed that the pains of Purgatory might be revealed to him. This request was granted and St. Patrick was much awed by the vision. On departing from the cave on this island he ordered that henceforth the island should be made a terrestrial purgatory where sinners could repent and atone in this world for their sins by prayer and fasting. Many saints and pious pilgrims imitated his example; the island in consequence is now called St. Patrick's Purgatory.

From the fifth until the close of the eighth century, Ireland won for herself among the nations the honourable distinction of being called the Insula Doctorum et Sanctorum – Isle of Saints and Scholars. It was her golden age, a time of teaching, a time of missions and missionaries, a time of building monasteries, colleges and schools. However, from the beginning of the ninth century to the time of the battle of Clontarf in 1014 the scene had much changed. The Danes had come and laid low most religious houses throughout the land. According to the Four Masters in the year 836 A.D., the churches of Lough Erne were destroyed by the Galls (Danish invaders) as were the churches of Clones and Devenish, all of them near by Lough Derg. Even supposing Lough Derg could have escaped pillage, the making of pilgrimage to St. Patrick's shrine in such times would have been a dangerous undertaking. Hence it is only to be expected that the sanctuary, if not completely demolished by the foreigners, was well nigh abandoned for a considerable period.

After the expulsion of the Danes from Ireland, the Augustinians came to Ireland. They took over ruined cloisters at Lough Derg, Devenish, Clones and many others. The Archbishop of Armagh is said to have asked them to come to Ireland about the year 1126, and placed the Abbey founded by himself at Armagh under their care. This Abbey was dedicated to Ss. Peter and Paul, as was the monastery on Saint's Island, Lough Derg, which was now occupied by those venerable canons. With their arrivals, the pilgrims to St. Patrick's sanctuary received a fresh welcome. The Augustinians continued in charge of Lough Derg for about five hundred years, from the twelfth century to the seventeenth century. Their expulsion came about 1632. From an inquisition taken at Donegal on 26th November, 1603, in the first year of the reign of James 1, it would appear that the Augustinians were driven from Lough Derg, and their church and monastery pulled down even before the year 1632. After the Augustinians came the Franciscan friars who stayed at Lough Derg until the close of the last century, when the Bishop of Clogher (in which diocese Lough Derg lies) appointed one of the secular priests of his diocese to officiate. Since then, under the care of the bishop and clergy of Clogher, Lough Derg has flourished as a pilgrimage. It has braved triumphantly many obstacles and enemies, and, after centuries of persecution, continues to be the proudest heritage of Ireland's faith and piety.

The remains of Termon crosses or standing stones which

123

marked a boundary of ecclesiastical endowment, are still to be found around the townlands bordering St. Patrick's Purgatory. To archaeologists, antiquarians or historians, indeed anyone whose right it is to preserve every iota of evidence of the past, and to clubs with such interests, it would be hard to find anywhere with such outlets for satisfying field-work.

'Let the terminus of a holy place have marks about it.

Wherever you find the sign of the Cross of Christ, do not do any injury.

Three persons consecrate a terminus or a holy place, a king, a bishop or the people'.

So, the lands bordering Lough Derg had such markings and a monument locally known as the 'Standing Stone' was really the pedestal of one of the termon crosses. Now as this pedestal or 'Standing Stone' has been broken up into fragments and is thus beyond the possibility of recognition or restoration it is fortunate that such an accurate description of it has been preserved. Thanks are due to the late Fr. Downey, who is long since gone to his everlasting reward. Here are Fr. Downey's details:

'The stone about which we talk is in the townland of Drumawark. It is a freestone, dressed pretty fairly, but has no inscriptions or characters upon it. It has four sides, is 2½ feet high, 2½ feet in depth, and 1½ feet in width, and stands in its original state. It was a pedestal for another stone which was removed from it either through bigotry, or mischief-making some twenty years ago, around the late 1850s. It was broken in almost equal halves, one of which lies about a hundred yards east of the pedestal. The other about the same distance to the west of it. The shaft appears to be of a harder kind of stone and more finely dressed than the pedestal'.

On the 15th of August, 1880, just as Lough Derg Station closed, the parish priest Rev. Fr. O'Connor, set out himself with two good friends. For his own interest, he wanted to examine this object of which Fr. Downey had given him the first reliable information, and also of testing the report of the destruction of the 'Standing Stone'. Canon O'Connor telling of his visit of investigation says:

"The afternoon was calm and sultry, not a ripple on the lake, and not a breath of air to sway the branches of the fir plantation, as we passed along through Ballymacaranny into the open country. Passing the crossroads where a bridge had been lately erected spanning the Owenea water, a tributary of the Termon river, we turned off to the left; and proceeded through the fields in the direction of Drumawark. We had not gone far when a thunderstorm burst upon the overhanging mountain Croagh Kinnagoe, accompanied by a downpour of hailstones which battered down the ripening crops in its destructive course. Soon the storm swept past and presently we heard the roar of the countless torrents leaping in wild career down the most precipitous slopes of the mountain. Having taken refuge at a vantage spot, we were soon enabled to continue our journey over partially submerged fields, and at length, we reached the anxiously sought hill of Drumawark. Lying in a ditch near the earthen fort that crowns the hill, we noticed a portion of the termon cross. It is finely chamfered at each angle of the front sides, but otherwise presents no ornamentation, having besides a tenon of about one foot in depth which must have fitted into the socket of the pedestal. Though only about one half of the original shaft, its weight cannot be less than three hundredweight. On top of the hillside overgrown with furze and heath, we observed on its summit a low earthwork of circular formation and not very spacious. It wants the fosse usually to be seen on forts throughout the country, and from the ring outward there is a deep declivity. Within its enclosures the soil seems rich and loamy, and in its centre at the time of Fr. Downey's visit, ten months previously, stood the 'Standing Stone', the position it occupied being now marked by an open pit in which lay broken fragments of that ancient monument. The motive for this dastardly vandal act is thus explained by concurrent testimony of several persons residing in the locality."

On the occasion of Father Downey's visit to the monolith, it was rumoured that the parts of the termon cross were to be collected together and re-erected on Station Island. To prevent such a step, certain narrow-minded folk came at dead night, equipped with spades, bars, sledge-hammers and lantern, dug a deep trench around the stone, broke it into fragments and there left them in the pit beyond all possibility of recognition. They then made their departure, leaving behind vivid traces of their savage work. On the night of this outrage a light was seen at the 'Standing Stone', and the strokes of a sledge-hammer were distinctly heard by several people. The tenant on the farm on which the monument stood was entirely exonerated from all complicity in the act, but suspicion, founded on certain grounds, pointed to the perpetrators of this regrettable deed. The stone top of the cross, 'like the wheel of a barrow', as the locals say, has for long marked a family grave in Templecrone churchyard. It is of red sandstone of the same sort as that found in most of the inscribed stones, crosses, and plaques at Lough Derg.

The storm which had overtaken Canon O'Connor on his mountain journey to see the 'Standing Stone', was the same storm which caused the tragedy at Gweedore — where several lives were lost by the flooding of Derrybeg chapel — mentioned earlier in this guide. It broke over Gweedore about three hours earlier that same day. To the brighter side of the picture, the views from the hill of Drumawark would excite any traveller or mountain hiker. From here the first glimpse of the Holy Lake is obtained by the tired and weary pilgrim, and from here also there is a very good view of Lough Erne extending from Enniskillen to Belleek. The monastic buildings of Devenish are clearly to be seen, where in times gone by, signal lights were known to have been the method of communicating messages between those two ecclesiastical stations. Macgrath's Castle near Pettigo can also be seen from Drumawark. This was the ancient residence of the guardian of the Termon lands bordering Lough Derg. There is a story of dreamers who believed gold could be found here, so they began digging deep into the eastern rim of this fort, hoping to strike fortune, but after much work all they came on was a regular floor or pavement of burnt stones, thought to have been a site where beacon fires were set, as well as where pilgrims cooked their frugal meals. About a quarter of a mile to the north-east of Drumawark is the holy well of Cullion, to which pilgrims, after completing their station at St. Patrick's Purgatory, Lough Derg, went to pay a visit, each one bringing with him from the shore of the lake, a rounded pebble which was left at the well as a votive gift. It is not quite certain what saint this well is dedicated to, it could be to the memory of St. Cillane who was an abbot of Lough Derg, and died in 721 A.D. There is a wee glen to the south of the well where, in the penal days, Mass used to be said.

There is but little change in the making of the station at Lough Derg, except that it takes but three days at the present time. Formerly the station lasted nine days, and earlier again it took fifteen days to complete its penitential exercises.

During settled weather Lough Derg wears an aspect pleasing to behold. At times its waters are hushed as in sleep, and not a ripple disturbs its placid surface. In such tranquil repose I have worked near its shores as a farmer's hired boy. Through the air rustles undescribable harmony. The crowing of a rooster from a distant farmyard sounds like a bugle note upon the ear, while the whir of moorfowl through the heather gives life and variety to a scene unique and charming.

To the south-east of the lake is the mountain, Croaghinnagoe, with an elevation of 1,194 feet, and Ardmore and Aughtadreen to the north, 1,086 feet and 1,071 feet respectively. Looking towards the north, the Cruacha Gorma mountains show off that blue hue of beauty, which they are so noted for, and looking westwards Slieve League can be seen, as it peers out, holding back as it were the sparkling waves of Donegal's broad bay. Rounding our gaze southwards the Sligo and Leitrim mountains meet our view, with those odd-looking, but well known cliffs of Benbulben, standing out like giant turf-stacks against the setting sun. To complete this unforgettable glory of sunset, we have nestling in peaceful solitude the Holy Lake, Lough Derg, with its famous islands — Station Island and Saint's Island, surrounded by many others, as if floating on its waters:

'So like a temple doth it stand
that there,
The hearts first impulse is to prayer.'

So, then, amid such a setting of mountain and moorland, St. Patrick's Shrine, Station Island, Lough Derg, present a singular, unique and pleasing picture. The neat churches, presbytery, hospice and various other buildings, from a distance look as if the island is completely occupied. Then the picture comes to life, when the viewer can catch a glimpse of crowds of fervent pilgrims moving about, much engaged in their devotional exercises, while the boats ply from the mainland to the island with coming and departing pilgrims. This is indeed a sight sacred and solemn, and so rare to the stranger as to make a deep impression on one's mind, and perhaps awaken in times to come pleasing memories of our rambles round Donegal.

Much, much more could be written of Lough Derg, its history, traditions, legends, antiquities, topography, and yet much more of its surroundings. However, to delve deeper in such a work would overload a traveller's guide, such as this, and no matter how much I would love to make such a holy place that much better known, I can at this point, but ask our tourists to come and see for themselves:

'The sacred stand our father's feet have often trod,
I nightly view,
The island of saints retreat,
Amid the mountains of Tirhugh.'